THE
ANXIOUS INQUIRER
AFTER SALVATION

THE

ANXIOUS INQUIRER
AFTER SALVATION
DIRECTED AND ENCOURAGED

"WHAT MUST I DO TO BE SAVED?"
"BELIEVE ON THE LORD JESUS CHRIST, AND YOU SHALL BE SAVED."
ACTS 16:30, 31

BY JOHN ANGELL JAMES, 1834

CCR
PUBLICATIONS

CHRIST CHURCH — RADFORD

THE ANXIOUS INQUIRER AFTER SALVATION
DIRECTED AND ENCOURAGED

CONTENTS

Preface

ALL subjects must be taught by elementary treatises: to this rule, religion forms no exception; and as books for children, compose a very useful, though humble department, in general literature, so in the great science of salvation, he aims at no unimportant object, who writes for those who are anxious to be converted, and who are willing, for that purpose, to become as little children in the school of Christ. Such is my design; to accomplish which, I sought after the greatest simplicity of style. Writing for babes in Christ, I have given little more than the alphabet of personal religion; but the learning of which is necessary to future progress. Almost all teachers, whether of children or of adults, commit the error of taking for granted, that their pupils know more than they really do: it is far better to err in the opposite extreme. If any are disposed to think I have carried my endeavors after simplicity too far, and are desirous of something more elaborate, I refer them to the excellent work of Dr. Henry, of Charleston, entitled, "Letters to a Friend," recommended by Dr. Pye Smith, the object of which is precisely the same as my own, but which is written in a more diffuse style, and illustrated by a greater variety of facts.

J. A. J.

Edgbaston, April, 1834.

INTRODUCTION

Directions

For *The Profitable Reading*
of The Following Treatise

IT may seem strange to some people, that I should give directions for the performance of an act so well understood as the perusal of a book; and especially the perusal of a book of so simple and elementary a kind as this. But the fact is, that multitudes either do not know, or do not at the time remember how to read to advantage; and, therefore, profit but little by what they read. Besides, simple and elementary as is this treatise, it is on a subject of infinite and eternal importance, and will be perused in the most critical season of a man's everlasting history; when, in a very peculiar sense, every means of grace, and this among the rest, will be either "a savor of death unto death, or of life unto life," to the reader. Tremendous idea! But strictly true.

Reader, whoever you are, you will remember the contents of this small treatise, either with pleasure and gratitude in heaven, or with remorse and despair in hell! Can it then be an impertinently officious act, to remind you how to read with advantage what I have written?

1. *Take it with you into your closet.* I mean your place of retirement for prayer; for, of course, you have such a place. Prayer is the very soul of all religion, and privacy is the very life of prayer itself. This is a book to be read when you are alone; when none is near but God and your conscience; when you are not hindered by the presence of a fellow-creature from the utmost freedom of manner, thought, and feeling; when, unobserved by any human eye, you can lay down the book, and meditate, or weep, or fall upon your knees to pray, or give vent to your feelings in short and sudden petitions to God. I charge you then to reserve this volume for your private seasons of devotion and thoughtfulness—look not into it in company, except it be the company of a poor trembling and anxious inquirer, like yourself.

2. *Read it with deep seriousness.* Remember, it speaks to you of God, of eternity, of salvation, of heaven, and of hell. Take it up with something of the awe, "that warns you how you touch a holy thing." It meets you in your solicitude about your soul's welfare; it meets you fleeing from destruction, escaping for your life, crying out, "What shall I do to be saved?" and offers its assistance to guide you for refuge to "the hope set before you in the gospel." It is itself serious; its Author is serious; it is on a serious subject; and demands to be read in a most devout and serious mood. Take it not up lightly, nor read it lightly. If your spirit be not as solemn as usual, do not touch it; and when you do touch it, put away every other subject, and endeavor to realize the idea that God, salvation, and eternity are before you; and that you are actually collecting the ingredients of the cup of salvation, or the wormwood and gall to embitter the cup of damnation!

3. *Read it with earnest prayer.* It can do you no good, without God's blessing—nothing short of Divine grace can render it the means of instructing your mind, or impressing your heart. It will convey no experimental knowledge, relieve no anxiety, dissipate no doubts, and afford neither peace nor

sanctification—if God does not give his Holy Spirit—and if you would have the Spirit, you must ask for his influence. If, therefore, you wish it to benefit you, do not read another page, until you have most fervently, as well as sincerely, prayed to God for his blessing to accompany the perusal. I have earnestly prayed to God to enable me to write it, and if you as earnestly pray to him to enable you to read it, there is thanksgiving in store for us both; for usually what is begun in prayer, ends in praise.

4. *Do not read too much at a time.* Books that are intended to instruct and impress should be read slowly. Most people read too much at a time. Your object is not merely to read this treatise through, but to read it so as to profit by it. Food cannot be digested well, if too much be eaten at a time; so neither can knowledge.

5. *Meditate on what you read.* Meditation bears the same office in the mental constitution, as digestion does in our corporeal system. The first mental exercise is attention, the next is reflection. If we would gain a correct notion of an object, we must not only see it, but look at it; and so, also, if we would gain knowledge from books, we must not only see the matters treated of, but steadily ponder them. Nothing but meditation can enable us to properly understand or feel. In reading the Scriptures and pious books, we are, or should be, reading for eternity. Salvation depends on knowledge, and knowledge on meditation. At almost every step of our progress through a book which is intended to guide us to salvation, we should pause and ask, "Do I understand this?" Our profiting depends not on the quantity we read, but the quantity we understand. One verse in Scripture, if understood and meditated upon, will do us more good than a chapter, or, even a book, read through in haste, and without reflection.

6. *Read regularly through in order.* Do not wander about from one part to another, and in your eagerness to gain relief,

pick and cull particular portions, on account of their supposed suitableness to your case. It is all suitable; and will be found most so by being taken together and as a whole. A rambling method of reading, whether it be the Scriptures or other books, is not to edification—it often arises from levity of mind, and sometimes from impatience; both of which are states very unfriendly to improvement. Remember it is salvation you are in quest of; an object of such transcendent importance, as to be a check upon volatility; and of such value, as to encourage the most exemplary patience.

7. *Read calmly.* You are anxious to obtain eternal life—you are eagerly asking, "What shall I do to be saved?" But still, you must not allow your solicitude so far to agitate your mind; as to prevent you from listening calmly and coolly for the answer. In circumstances of great concern, men are sometimes so much under the power of excited feelings, that their judgment is bewildered, and thus they are not only prevented from finding out what is best to be done, but from seeing it when it is laid down by another. This anxious and hurried state of mind is very common in those who are just awakened to a concern about salvation; they are restless and eager to gain relief, but are defeated in their object by their very solicitude to obtain it. The Scriptures are read, sermons are heard, advice of friends is received, in a confused state of mind. Now you must guard against this, and endeavor so far to control your thoughts, and calm your perturbation as to attend to the counsels and cautions which are here suggested.

8. *I very earnestly recommend the perusal of all those passages of Scripture and chapters which I have quoted, and which, for the sake of brevity, I have only referred to, without quoting the words.* I lay great stress upon this. Read this book with the Bible at your elbow, and do not think much of the trouble of turning to the passages quoted. If, unhappily, you should consider me, or my little volume, as a substitute for the Bible, instead of a guide to it, I shall have done you an injury,

or rather you will have done yourself an injury by thus employing it. "As new-born babes," says the apostle, "desire the sincere milk of the word, that you may grow thereby." And as those infants thrive best who are fed from the bosom of their mothers, so those converts grow most in grace, who are most devoted to a spiritual perusal of the Scriptures. If, therefore, I stand between you and the word of God, I do you great disservice; but if I should persuade you to read the Scriptures, I shall greatly help you in your pious course. Perhaps, in the present state of your mind, it is not desirable to begin and read regularly the word of God, but to go through those passages which I have selected and recommended.

And now may God, of his great goodness and sovereign grace, deign to bless the perusal of this book to many immortal souls, by making it, however humble the production, the means of conducting them into the path of life!

CHAPTER ONE

Deep Solicitude about Salvation,
Reasonable and Necessary

READER, you have lately been awakened, by the mercy of God, to ask, with some degree of concern, that momentous question, *"What shall I do to be saved?"* No wonder you are concerned; the wonder is, that you were not concerned about this matter before, that you are not more deeply solicitous now, and that all who possess the word of God do not sympathize with you in this concern. Everything justifies solicitude, and condemns indifference as to this matter. Unconcern about the soul, indifference to salvation, is a most irrational as well as a most guilty state of mind. The wildest enthusiasm about these matters is less surprising and unreasonable than absolute carelessness, as will appear from the following considerations.

1. *Reader! You are an immortal creature, a being born for eternity, a creature that will never go out of existence.* Millions of ages, as numerous as the sands upon the shore, and the drops of the ocean, and the leaves of all the forests on the globe, will not shorten the duration of your existence. Eternity, vast eternity, incomprehensible eternity, is before you! Every day brings you nearer to everlasting torments or felicity. You

may die any moment—and you are as near to heaven or hell as you are to death. No wonder you are asking, "What shall I do to be saved?"

2. But the reasonableness of this concern appears, *if you add to this consideration, that you are a sinner.* You have broken God's law; you have rebelled against his authority; you have acted as an enemy to him, and made him *your* enemy. If you had committed only one single act of transgression, your situation would be alarming. *One* sin would have subjected you to the sentence of his law, and exposed you to his displeasure; but you have committed sins more in number, and greater in magnitude, than you know, or can conceive of. Your whole life has been one continued sin—you have, so far as God is considered, done nothing but sin. Your transgressions have sent up to heaven a cry for vengeance. You are actually under the curse of the Almighty!

3. *Consider what the loss of the soul includes.* The loss of the soul is the loss of everything dear to man as an immortal creature—it is the loss of heaven, with all its honors, felicities, and glories; it is the loss of God's favor, which is the life of all rational creatures; it is the loss of everything that can contribute to our happiness; and it is the loss of hope, the last refuge of the wretched. The loss of the soul includes in it all that is contained in that dreadful, word, *Hell.* Hell is the eternal endurance of the wrath of God; it is the coming down of the curse of the Almighty upon the human spirit; or rather, it is the falling of the human spirit into that curse, as into a lake that burns with fire and brimstone. How true, as well as solemn, are the words of Christ, *"What shall it profit a man, if he gains the whole world and loses his own soul; or what shall a man give in exchange for his soul?"* All the tears that ever have been or ever will be shed on the face of the earth, all the groans that ever have been or ever will be uttered, all the anguish that ever has been or ever will be endured by all the inhabitants of the

world, through all the ages of time, do not make up an equal amount of misery to that which is included in the loss of one human soul. Justly therefore do you say, who are exposed to this misery, *"What shall I do to be saved?"*

4. This solicitude is reasonable *if you consider that the eternal loss of the soul is not a rare, but a very common occurrence.* It is so tremendous a catastrophe, that if it happened only once in a year, or once in a century, so as to render it barely possible that it should happen to you, it would be reckless carelessness not to feel some solicitude about the matter—how much more, then, when, alas! it is an every-day calamity! So far from its being a rare thing for men to go to hell, it is a much rarer thing for them to go to heaven. Our Lord tells us, that the road to destruction is thronged, while the way to life is traveled by few. Hell opens its mouth wide and swallows up multitudes in perdition! How alarming is the idea, and how probable the fact, that you may be among this number! Some who read these pages will very likely spend their eternity in hell. It is therefore your wisdom, as well as your duty, to cherish the concern which says, "What shall I do to be saved?"

5. *Salvation* is possible, for if it were not, it would be useless to be concerned about it. It would be cruel to encourage a concern which could never be relieved by the possession of the object which excites it. But *your* case is not hopeless; you *may* be saved; you are invited to be saved. Christ has died for your salvation, and God waits to save you; all the opportunities, advantages, helps, and encouragements to salvation are round you; the blessing is within your reach; it is brought near to you; and it will be your own fault if you do not possess it. Your solicitude is not therefore directed to an unattainable object.

6. *Salvation has been obtained by multitudes, and why may it not be obtained by you?* Millions in heaven are already saved; myriads more are on the road to salvation. God is still

as willing, and Christ is still as able, to save you as he was them—why, then, should not you be saved?

7. *And then what a blessing is salvation!* A blessing that includes all the riches of grace, and all the greater riches of glory; deliverance from sin, death, and hell; the possession of pardon, peace, holiness, and heaven; a blessing immense, infinite, everlasting; which occupied the mind of Deity from eternity, was procured by the Son of God upon the cross, and will fill eternity with its happiness. Oh, how little, insignificant, and contemptible is the highest object of human ambition, to say nothing of the lower matters of men's desires, compared with salvation! Riches, rank, fame, and honors, are but as the small dust of the balance, when compared with the "salvation which is in Christ Jesus with eternal glory." Who that pretends to the least regard to his own happiness would not say, "What shall I do to be saved?"

8. *The circumstances in which you are placed for obtaining this blessing are partly favorable—and partly unfavorable.* The love of God is infinite; the merit of Christ is infinite; the power of the Holy Spirit is infinite—Jehovah is willing and waiting to save you; Christ invites; all things are ready, and the grace of God offered for your conversion. On the other hand, you have a corrupt heart, and are placed in a world where everything seems to combine to draw off your attention from salvation, and to cause you to neglect it. Satan is busy to blind your mind; the world, to fill your imagination and heart with other objects, so that even the "righteous are *scarcely* saved." You cannot leave the world, and go into monasteries and convents, but must seek salvation amidst the engrossing cares of this busy and troublesome world; where concern about the body is so liable to put away concern about the soul, and things seen and temporal are likely to withdraw the attention from things that are unseen and eternal. Oh, how difficult it is to pay just enough regard to present things, and yet not too

much! How difficult to attend properly to the affairs both of earth and heaven; to be busy for two worlds at once! These circumstances may well excite your solicitude.

Concern, then, deep concern about salvation, is the most reasonable thing in the world; and I feel almost ready to ask, Can that man have a soul, or know that he has one, who is careless about its eternal happiness? Is he a man or a brute? Is he in the exercise of his reason, or is he a maniac? Ever walking on the edge of the precipice that hangs over the bottomless pit—and not concerned about salvation! Oh, fatal, awful, destructive indifference! Nourish, then, *your* solicitude. You *must* be concerned, you *ought* to be so, you *cannot be saved without it;* for no man ever was, or ever will be. The salvation of a lost soul is such a stupendous deliverance, such an infinitely momentous concern, that it is impossible, in the very nature of things, it should be bestowed on anyone who is not in earnest to obtain it. This is the very end of your existence, the purpose for which God created you. Apart from this, you are an enigma in creation; a mystery in nature. Why has God given you faculties which seem to point to eternity, and desires which go forward to it—if he has not destined you for it? Eternal salvation is the great end of life—get what you will, if you lose your soul, you have lost the purpose of existence. Could you obtain all the wealth of the globe; could you rise to the possession of universal empire; could you, by the most splendid discoveries in science, or the most useful inventions in art, or the most magnificent achievements in literature, fill the earth with the fame of your exploits, and send down your name with honor to the last ages of time, still, if you lost the salvation of your soul, you would have lived in vain! Whatever you may gain, life will be a lost adventure, if you do not gain salvation. The condition of the poorest creature who ever obtained eternal life through faith in Jesus Christ, although he had but a mere glimmering of intellect, just enough of understanding to apprehend the nature of repentance, although he lived out his days amidst the most squalid poverty and repulsive scenes, although he was unknown even among the poor, and although, when he died, he was buried in a pauper's grave, on which no tear is shed—is infinitely to be preferred to that of the most successful merchant, the greatest conqueror, the profoundest philosopher, or the sublimest poet, that ever existed—if he lived and died without salvation. The lowest place in heaven is infinitely to be preferred to the highest place on earth!

Go on, then, to urge the question, *"What shall I do to be saved?"* Let no one turn off your attention from this matter. As long as you covet this, your eye, and heart, and hope are fixed on the sublimest object in the universe; and when meddlesome but ignorant friends would persuade you that you are too concerned, point them to the bottomless pit, and ask them if anyone *can* be too anxious to escape its torments? Point them to heaven, and ask them if anyone can be too anxious to obtain its glories? Point them to eternity, and ask them if anyone can be too anxious to secure immortal life? Point them to the cross of Christ, and ask them if anyone can be too anxious to secure the object for which he died?

CHAPTER TWO

Religious Impressions,
and the Importance of Retaining and Deepening Them

AWAKENED and anxious sinner, your present situation is a most momentous one. You are in the crisis of your religious history and of your eternal destiny. No tongue can tell, no pen describe, the importance of your present circumstances. You are just arousing from your long slumber of sin and spiritual death, and will now either rise up and run the race that is set before you, or will soon sink back again (as those are likely to do who are only a little disturbed) into a deeper sleep than ever. The Spirit of God is striving with you, and either you will yield to his suggestions, and give yourself up to be led by his gracious influence—or you will grieve him by resistance and neglect, and cause him to depart. God is drawing you with the cords of love; Christ is saying, "Behold, I stand at the door, and knock;" the Spirit is striving with you. Yield to these silken bands; open to that gracious Savior; grieve not, quench not the motions of that Divine Spirit. Salvation is come near, and heaven is opening to your soul.

Remember, you may quench the Spirit, not only by direct resistance, but by careless neglect. Do not, I beseech you, be insensible to your situation. A single conviction ought not to be treated with indifference, or a single impression to be overlooked. You cannot long remain as you now are; your convictions will soon end either in conversion—or in greater indifference. Like the blossoms of spring, they will soon set in fruit—or fall to the ground. Should your present solicitude diminish, it will soon subside altogether; and if it subsides, it may probably never be revived. It is a most dangerous thing to tamper or trifle with convictions of sin and religious impressions. If, then, you would *not* lose your present feelings, take the following advice:

1. Admit the *possibility* of losing them. Do not presume that it is impossible for *you* to relapse. Let there be no approach to the vain-glorious, self-confident temper of the apostle Peter, who said, "Although all should fall away, I never will." Nothing is more common than mere transient devotions. The character of Pliable in the "Pilgrim's Progress," is one of every day's occurrence. There are very few that hear the gospel, who are not, at one time or other, the subject of religious impressions. Multitudes, who are lifting up their eyes in torment, are looking back upon lost impressions! Do not conclude that, because you are now so concerned about salvation, that you *must* be saved. Oh no. Many that read these pages under deep solicitude, will add to the number of backsliders. Self-confidence will be sure to end in confusion; while self-distrust is the way to stand.

2. *Dread the idea of relapsing into indifference.* Let the bare thought of indifference make you tremble. Exclaim almost in an agony of spirit, "Oh, if I should prove treacherous; if my goodness should be as the morning cloud or early dew; if this heart of *mine*, which now seems so much in earnest, should become indifferent; if my soul, which now seems not far from the kingdom of God, should go back from its very gates, and walk the ways of God no more; if my friends or

minister should meet me in a retreating course, and have to say to me, 'You did run well, what has hindered you?' Dreadful change! may God in mercy prevent it."

My dear reader, let these be your reflections. Let death seem to you to be coveted, rather than backsliding; let it be your feeling that you would rather go forward in the pursuit of salvation, though you were to die the moment your sins were pardoned, than gain long life and the whole world, by going back to indifference. Next to the loss of the soul, there is nothing so dreadful in itself, nor so much to be dreaded, as the loss of religious impressions; and the latter leads on to the former.

3. *Make it a subject of devout and earnest prayer that God would render your impressions permanent, by the effectual aid of his Holy Spirit.* Reader, here learn these two lessons; that God alone can seal these emotions upon your heart, and that he can be expected to do it only in answer to prayer. It is of infinite consequence that you should, at this stage of your religious history, deeply ponder the great truth—that all true piety in the heart of man is the work of God's Spirit. Do not read another line until you have well weighed that sentiment, and have so wrought it into your heart, as to make it with you a principle of action, and a rule of conduct. Every conviction will be extinguished, every impression will be effaced—unless God himself, by his own sovereign and efficacious grace, renders them permanent. If God does not put forth his power, you will as certainly lose every pious emotion. You may as rationally expect light without the sun—as piety without God. Not a single truly holy feeling will ever come into the mind, or be kept there, but by God. Hence, the object and use of prayer are to obtain this gracious influence.

Prayer is the first step in the divine life, prayer is the second step in the divine life, prayer is the third step in the divine life. And indeed prayer is necessary through the whole Christian course. Awakened sinner, you must *pray*. You *must* find opportunity to be alone; you must cry mightily unto God; you must *implore* his aid; you must give up a portion of your sleep —if you can command no time in the day for prayer. In one sense, you should pray always. The spirit of prayer should dwell in you and never depart, and be continually leading you to spontaneous petitions in the house and by the way, upon your bed and in your occupations; and *this* should be the subject of your petitions, that your impressions may not be permitted to die away, but go on to conversion. You may read books, consult friends, hear sermons, and make resolutions; but books, friends, sermons, and resolutions will all fail—if God does not give his Holy Spirit. It is very common for beginners to trust too much to means, and too little to God. If you *will* not, or even if you suppose you *cannot*, find time for private prayer, you may as well stop at once, and give up the pursuit of salvation—for you cannot be saved without it.

4. If you would retain your impressions and persevere in the pursuit of salvation, *you must at once determine to give up whatever you know to be sinful in your conduct, and you must also be very watchful against sin.* Thus runs the direction of the word of God—"Seek the Lord while he may be found, call you upon him while he is near—*let the wicked forsake his way, and the unrighteous man his thoughts*; and let him return unto the Lord, and he will have mercy upon him, and to our God, for he will abundantly pardon." To the same effect is the language of one of Job's friends—"If you prepare your heart, and stretch out your hands toward him; if iniquity be in your hand, put it far away."

It is right for you at once to know, that the salvation which is in Christ is a deliverance *from* sin. "You shall call his name Jesus, for he shall save his people *from* their sins," said the angel to Joseph, when he announced the approaching nativity of Christ. "Who gave himself for us, that he might redeem us from all iniquity, and purify unto himself a peculiar people, zealous of good works." It is of immense consequence that you should at once have a distinct idea that the salvation you are beginning to seek, is a holy calling. Whatever is sinful in your temper, such as malice, revenge, violent passions; or whatever is sinful in your words, in the way of falsehood, railing, back-biting; or whatever is sinful in your practice, in the way of in-justice, unkindness, undutifulness to parents or masters; must immediately be given up without hesitation, reluctance, or re-serve.

The retaining of one single sin, which you know to be such, will soon stifle your convictions, and efface all your im-pressions. If you are not willing to give up your sins, it is not Christian salvation you are seeking. You may suppose you wish to become a Christian, and read the Bible, offer up prayers, and regularly hear sermons, and you wonder that you do not get on in religion. But perhaps the reason is, you are not willing to give up your sins, your worldly-mindedness, your carnal pleasures, or some practice that you find to be gainful or agreeable, although you know it to be sinful. Well, then, you cannot get on in this state of mind. Do, do, therefore, look carefully within; examine faithfully your conduct, and see whether there be in you anything which you know to be wrong, but which you are nevertheless unwilling to abandon—if there is, it is vain for you to think of retaining your impres-sions, and becoming a Christian.

And let me also remind you, that this willingness to give up your sins must be immediate; you must desire and propose an instant abandonment of sin. Augustine confesses that he used to pray to God to convert him, but with this reservation, "Lord, not yet." He wished to live a little longer in the gratifi-cation of his sinful lusts, before he was completely turned to the Lord from his evil ways. Thus there are some who are, or profess to be, desirous to be converted at some time or other, and who are willing to give up their sins, but "not yet." There is a mixture of feeling; a concern to be saved, but a lingering love of some sin; and the matter is settled by a resolution to sacrifice the sin at some future time. Awful delusion! God says, *"Now!"* and you must reply, "Yes, Lord, now; I would *now* be converted from this and every sin."

And not only must you be willing *to give up sin,* but you must *watch most carefully against* it. You are in a most critical state of mind; and a very small indulgence of sin may put away all your pious feelings. Even the giving way to a bad temper may do irreparable mischief to your soul, and hinder your pursuit of eternal life. You ought especially to watch against your besetting sin, whatever it is, according to the exhortation of the apostle (Heb. 12:1). At the same time I would caution you against being discouraged by occasional failures; you are not to throw up all in despair because you are occasionally overcome by temptation. Instances of this kind should make you more watchful, but not desponding. I shall say more on this subject hereafter.

5. *It is of great consequence for you to separate yourselves from unholy or worldly companions.* It will require some courage, and call for some painful self-denial, to retire from the society of those with whom you have been in the habit of associating; but if they are ungodly people, *it must be done.* Read what God and godly men have said on this subject (Psalm 119:63; Prov. 1:11-16; 2:12-19; 29:6; 13:20; 1 Cor. 15:33; 2 Cor. 6:14-18). Comply with these admonitions, and leave the society of all who think lightly of true religion. Their company and conversation will soon draw you aside from the ways of piety. Their levity, their indifference, their neglect of salvation, will be destructive to all your pious feelings. Even Christians of long standing and of deeply-rooted piety find such society very unfriendly to their godliness, and avoid it as much as possible—how much more dangerous will it be to

you, whose religion is yet so feeble and incapable of much opposition! Even if such companions do not attempt to laugh or reason you out of your concern for your soul, (which, however, they will be almost sure to do, and never cease until they have succeeded,) their very conversation and general disposition will wither your tender piety, as an east wind does the blossoms of spring. *You must then give up either your sinful associates—or your salvation*; for if you cannot, or rather *will* not break off from such companions as are opposed to true religion, you may as well relinquish all hope of eternal life, since the preservation of pious feeling, and communion with the ungodly, are utterly incompatible with each other. Is there any companion on earth whose friendship you prefer to salvation, and whose loss you dread more than damnation?

6. *It is transcendently important that you should use all those scriptural means which are calculated and intended to keep up a due sense of piety in the mind.* These you must immediately and most earnestly employ—no time must be lost, no labor must be spared, no sacrifice must be grudged. Your soul and all her eternal interests are at stake. Hell is to be escaped; heaven is to be sought; Satan is to be conquered; salvation is to be obtained. Your enemies are numerous and mighty; your difficulties are immense, though not insurmountable. Every energy must be roused, every exertion must be made, every help called in, every lawful means employed. Read the following passages of God's word, and see if religion be a light and easy work. "Seek *first* the kingdom of God, and his righteousness." "*Strive* to enter in at the strait gate; for many, I say unto you, will seek to enter in, and shall not be able." "*Labor* for that food which endures unto eternal life." "Fight the good fight of faith, lay hold on eternal life." "Whoever will come after me, let him deny himself, and take up his cross, and follow me."

What metaphors! What language! We might almost feel prompted to ask, Who then can be saved—if such concern, such effort be necessary? Even the righteous are scarcely saved. If you do not, like David, seek the favor of God with *your whole heart,* you will never have it. You may more rationally think to reach the top of the highest mountain on earth without labor, than to imagine you can reach heaven without effort. If you suppose a *few wishes* or a *little exertion* will do, you are mistaken; and the sooner you are undeceived the better. But I will now specify the means you should use.

Immediately commence the devout and diligent perusal of the Scriptures. "As new-born babes, desire the sincere milk of the word, that you may grow thereby." The Bible is the food of the soul, even as the mother's milk is the nourishment of the child; and you may as easily believe that the infant will grow without food, as that you will grow in knowledge of grace without the Scriptures. Read for both instruction and for impression; read attentively, and with meditation; pause and ponder as you go along. Neglect not the book of God for the books of men—the latter may be read as the interpreters, but not as the substitutes of the former. If you do not find the Bible so interesting to you at first as you expected and wished, still go on; it will grow upon acquaintance. Nothing is so likely to keep up and to deepen religious impressions, as the serious perusal of the Scriptures; they are the very element of devotion. Of two inquirers after salvation, *he* will be most likely to persevere and to grow in piety, who is most diligent in reading the word of God. Do not be disheartened by finding much that you cannot at present understand; there is much that you can understand. *Read in course,* but instead of beginning the Bible, take the Psalms, the Gospels, and the Epistles, and make these the first portion of your study.

Attend with regularity and seriousness upon the preaching of the gospel. Sermons are invaluable helps to the anxious inquirer. Hear the word preached, with a deep conviction that it will do you no good but as God blesses it, and therefore look above the minister to God. Pray before you go to hear sermons; pray while you hear; and pray after you have heard. Go from the closet of private prayer to the place of public worship, and from the place of public worship back again to prayer. Apply the word as you hear it to yourself; hear with attention, hear as for yourself, hear as for salvation. Avoid a light and careless way of attending upon the means of grace. Grow not sinfully familiar with sacred things. Avoid general light conversation after sermons; and gratify not those evil spirits who desire to steal away the good seed of the word from the hearts in which it has been sown.

If you have the opportunity, avail yourselves of the advantages of *social prayer*. The prayers of good men are like gentle breezes to fan the spark of piety in the young convert's heart, and to surround him with the atmosphere of devotion. In these meetings you will be prayed with and prayed for—you will hear what more advanced Christians feel and desire, and their prayers are some of the best instructions you can receive—*thus* you will have your hearts knit together in love with the people of God.

You should seek the instructions and counsels of some pious friend, with whom you should be free and full in laying open the state of your mind. Frequent the company of the righteous, and at once identify yourself with them. You must not be ashamed to let your attachment to his cause and your adherence to his people be openly known. Many people wish to come and make *secret* peace with God, because fear, or pride, or self-interest, remonstrates against an open admission of his claims. They keep their convictions to themselves, and hence they sometimes soon die away for lack of support.

But it is especially desirable, that you should make known your mind to your minister. Go, without delay, to him. Perhaps he has meetings for inquirers, and even if he has not, he will no doubt be glad to hear your account of yourselves, and will tenderly sympathize with you under your anxieties. If he is like his Divine Master, he will "gather the lambs of the flock in his arms, carry them in his bosom, and gently lead those that are with young." Be not afraid to go to him if you are timid, and unable to say much, he will understand your broken hints, kindly elicit your sentiments and feelings, and give you suitable instruction and encouragement. One half-hour's conversation with a skillful physician of souls will often do more to assist you in this first stage of your religious history, than the reading of many books, and the hearing of many sermons.

Remember, however, after all there is a danger of depending too much upon means, as well as of too much neglecting them. Forget not what I have said concerning the work of the Spirit of God. *He* is your Helper, neither friends nor minister, neither reading nor hearing, no, nor the Bible itself, must lead you away from your dependence on the Holy Spirit. Many inquirers seem to have no hope or expectation of good but in connection with certain means; if they are cut off from sermons even occasionally, or have not precisely the same number and kind of ordinances they have been accustomed to, they are gloomy and desponding, fretful and peevish, and hence do not only get no good, but much harm by their unbelief and bad temper. We must depend upon God, and upon nothing but God, who could bless his people in the darkness of a dungeon, where the Bible could not be read, or in the solitude of a wilderness, where no gospel sermon could be heard.

It is of consequence that you should here distinctly understand, that the grace of God in your salvation is rich and free. Your exertions in seeking salvation do not merit or deserve it; and if you receive it, you will not have it granted to you as the reward of your own efforts to obtain it. To imagine that you can claim the grace that is necessary to your conversion, because you profess to seek it, is to follow the wretched example of those who, in ancient times, went "about to establish their own righteousness, and did not submit themselves unto the righteousness of God." Your deep convictions, impressions, and solicitude, your many tears, your earnest prayers, your diligent attendance upon sermons, and your partial reformations, can claim nothing in the way of reward from Him; nor is he bound to save you for that which has no reference to his glory—until you believe God's promise, he is under no obligation, even to himself, to save you. Notwithstanding all your concern and endeavors, you lie at his mercy; and if you are saved, it is because of the pure favor and grace of God.

Do not allow yourself to conclude, that your present concern is sure to end in the conversion of your soul to God. Nothing is more likely to deaden and even to destroy religious impressions, than to infer that you are sure of being converted because you are concerned about it; facts are against such an inference.

I have read of a gentleman, who felt, in a dangerous sickness, great horror at the review of his past life, and was advised to send for the minister of the parish, that he might set his mind at rest. The minister came. The gentleman told him that if God would be pleased to preserve him from death, his life should be the reverse of what it had been. He would regularly attend church; he would catechize his servants; he would regularly worship God in his family and in his closet; he would, in short, do everything a good Christian should do. His wishes were accomplished; he was thankful for his deliverance, and did not forget his promises. For many months he continued, as far as his conduct could be judged of by the world, to perform his vows. After a time, however; he thought so much religion superfluous. He first left off the duties of the closet and family; *public* duties at last became likewise too wearisome, and he became again the same man that he former- ly was. After some time, he was again seized by a dangerous distemper, and was advised by his friends to send again for the minister, that he might afford fresh consolation to his wounded spirit. "No," said he, "after breaking all the promises that I made to God, I cannot expect mercy from him." Death found him in this unhappy state of mind, and carried him to that world where there are no changes.

This story, with some variations of no consequence, may be told of myriads. Impressions are made upon the minds of sinners, which are attended with visible consequences, that give rise to favorable hopes in the bosoms of friends and min- isters; but their hopes often prove illusions. "When the Lord slew the children of Israel, then they sought him; and they re- turned and inquired early after God—and they remembered that God had been their Rock, and the high God their Re- deemer; nevertheless they flattered him with their mouths, and lied unto him with their tongues." (Psalm 78:35) They did not intentionally lie. They seem frequently to have been sincere at the time in their promises; not, indeed, with a godly sincerity —"yet *their hearts were not right with God*, neither were they steadfast in his covenant," and the reason why they were not steadfast in his covenant was, because, though they were im- pressed, their hearts were not right with God.

Perhaps there is no minister of the gospel who could not furnish some most affecting illustrations of the sentiment, that impressions and convictions do not always end in conversion. I began my own religious course with three companions, one of whom was materially serviceable, in some particulars, to my- self; but he soon proved that *his* religion was nothing more than mere transient devotion. A second returned to his sin, "like a dog to his vomit, and a pig that is washed to her wal- lowing in the mire." The third, who was for some time my inti- mate friend, imbibed the principles of infidelity; and so great was his zeal for his new creed, that he sat up at night to copy out Paine's "Age of Reason." After a while he was seized with a dangerous disease; his conscience awoke; the convictions of his mind were agonizing; his remorse was horrible. He ordered all his infidel extracts, that had cost him so many nights to copy out, to be burnt before his face—and if not in words, yet in spirit,

> *"Burn, burn," he cried, "in sacred rage,*
> *Hell is the due of every page."*

His infidel companions and his infidel principles forsook him at once, and in the hearing of a pious friend who visited him, and to whom he confessed with tears and lamentations his backsliding, he uttered his confessions of sin, and his vows of repentance. He recovered; but, painful to relate, it was only to relapse again, if not into infidelity, yet at any rate into an utter disregard to true religion.

These are awful instances, and prove by facts, which are unanswerable arguments, that it is but too certain that many seek to enter in at the strait gate, but do not accomplish their object. And why? Not because God is unwilling to save them, but because they rest in impressions, without going on to actual conversion. It is dangerous then, reader, as well as unwarranted, to conclude that you are sure to be saved. It is very true that where God has begun a good work he will carry it on to the day of Jesus Christ; but do not conclude too certainly that he has begun it. You may take encouragement from your present state of mind to hope that you will be saved; but that encouragement should rather come from what God has promised, and what God is, than from what you feel. To regard your present state of mind, therefore, with delight; to conceive of it as preferring any claim upon God to convert you; to look upon it as affording a certainty that you will be ultimately converted, a kind of pledge of salvation, instead of considering it only as struggles after salvation, which may or may not be successful, according as they are continued in a right manner; is the way to lose the impressions themselves, and to turn back again to sin or the world. The true light in which to consider your present solicitude is that of a state of mind which, if it terminates in genuine faith, and which it is probable it may, will end in your salvation. Consequently, your object should be to cherish your concern, and seek the grace of Jehovah to give you sincere repentance towards God, and true faith in our Lord Jesus Christ.

The subject of this chapter may be illustrated and enforced, by an extract from that admirable and most edifying book, "The Diary of Mr. Joseph Williams, of Kidderminster." "About this time," he says, when speaking of his youthful days, "going with my father a few miles from home, his talk with me was very profitable. He exhorted me to serious religion now in my youth, as the season when the mind is most fit to receive good impressions. He cautioned me not to put off the grand concern to an uncertain hereafter. He pleaded with me, not only the uncertainty of life, but the improbability of my turning to God in old age, after wicked habits were grown strong by a long continuance in sin. To affect me the more, he gave me the following particulars of his conversation with a gentleman of his acquaintance. I was coming home, said he, one evening, from Bewdley, in company with Mr. Radford and his son John. After he had related to me some particulars in his conduct, in vindicating some persecuted Christians against an unkind attack, he directed his discourse to his son. 'Son,' said he, 'though I have not myself been so religious and careful of my soul as I should have been, yet I cannot but have a tender concern for your everlasting happiness; and here, before Mr. Williams, I admonish you not to live after my example. I have often advised you to make this man your associate, he will lead you in the way to heaven. You are got in with a group of young fellows who will do you no good; but I charge you,' which he uttered with a louder voice, 'to leave off the company of such and such, and spend all the time you can in the company of this neighbor.' To which I replied, 'Sir, I am now full of business, and am much older than your son, therefore young men of his own age are more fit for him to associate with.' On my saying this, he stopped his horse, I being before him, and his son behind him; then, with great earnestness, he declared to him, 'I will not stir from this place until you have promised me to abandon that set of companions, and make this man your daily associate. Mind true religion in your youth; and do not do as I have done. I have slighted many convictions, and now my heart is hard and brawny.' I was in a manner thunderstruck with the old gentleman's last words. My thoughts were wholly swallowed up in deep musing on these words, 'My heart is hard and brawny.' I had such an affecting sense of the old gentleman's dreadful state, that it engaged my mind all the rest of the way; and even while I was transacting business, it was uppermost; for his words were ever sounding in my ears. Thus I was kept long in a very serious frame; and was possessed with a most alarming fear lest I should fall into such a state, which I considered as the greatest plague that could be inflicted on me. In this temper of mind I returned home, keeping my thoughts all the way intent upon the sad and solemn subject. While I was musing, the fire burned, my heart was hot within me, and I kept up a serious soliloquy on the most important concerns of my soul; and the impressions did not wear off for a considerable time."

CHAPTER THREE

On the Importance of Gaining Scriptural Knowledge,
and Clear Views of Divine Truth

THERE is scarcely anyone point to which the attention of anxious inquirers should be more earnestly and carefully directed, than the necessity of an accurate understanding of the plan of salvation, and the fundamental doctrines of the Scripture. You must endeavor to have clear ideas, correct views, precise and intelligent notions. The concern of many people is nothing more than an ignorant concern to be religious; they have scarcely one definite idea what religion is. Others are a little better informed than this, but still have no notion of piety, but as either a state of excited feeling, or a course of external religious observances. It is important that you should perceive that the whole superstructure of personal godliness rests on knowledge. True conversion is emphatically called, "coming to the *knowledge* of the truth." Your impressions will be easily effaced, and your concern will soon subside, if you do not give yourself time, and use means to become acquainted with the truth. There is much to be learned and known—as well as to be felt and done—and you cannot either feel or act aright, unless you do learn it. The reason why so many turn back, and others go on so slowly, is, because *they do not study to make themselves acquainted with Divine truth.*

Suppose a man were traveling through a strange country, could he get on without consulting his map? Would it be of any service to wish he could travel faster, and get on better, if he never looked at his map of roads? How can you get on in the way to heaven, without studying the Bible, which is the map of the road? Or, changing the illustration, suppose you were in financial difficulties, and some friend had told you not only how to extricate yourself from your perplexities, but also how to acquire great wealth; and in order to guard you from error, had given you long written directions. What would you do? Sit down, and wish and long for success, and immediately set out in a great bustle to realize the promised advantages? No. You would say, "My success depends upon knowledge, upon my making myself accurately acquainted with the particulars of my friend's written directions. I will read them, therefore, with the greatest care, until I have everyone of his ideas in my mind; for it is quite useless to exert myself, if I do not know how my exertions are to be directed."

This you confess is quite rational; and is it not quite as necessary for *you* to be acquainted with the subject of religion, in order to be truly pious? Knowledge, knowledge, my friends, is indispensable. True religion is repentance towards God; but *can* you repent if you do not know the character of the God whom you have offended, the law you have broken, and the sin you have committed? True religion is faith in our Lord Jesus Christ; but *can* you *really believe,* if you do not know whom and what you are to believe? True religion is the love of God; but can you love a being whom you do not *know*? You must give yourself, therefore, time and opportunity for reflection; you must bring your understanding to the business; you must study religion as a science to be known, as well as a passion to be felt, or a rule to be observed. It is of great consequence that, at this stage of your progress, you should clearly understand, that it is an obvious law of the human mind, that neither faith nor feeling of any kind can be produced by any other means than that of knowledge. Suppose you want to believe a person, or love him, or rejoice in him—can you work up yourself to do so unless you have some reason for it? No; you must know some grounds on which you can credit him, and some excellencies which render him worthy of your affection, and some facts which are a just cause of joy. No passion or affection can be called into exercise but by the knowledge of something that is calculated to excite it. You may try as long as you please to work upon your mind otherwise, but the thing is manifestly impossible.

Hence, then, the importance of growing in knowledge of Divine things. The way to have your faith increased, is to increase in the knowledge of what is to be believed—and if you would be rooted and grounded in love, you must be first rooted and grounded in the knowledge of what you are to love. The order of nature is, first to *know, then* to feel, then to act; and grace follows the order of nature. I deduce, therefore, this inference, t*hat in the whole business of religion, the eye of the inquirer must be much fixed on objects out of himself,* on those that are presented in the word of God. If you ask what are the subjects which you should endeavor to understand, I place before you the following—

1. *The moral character of God.* The knowledge of God is the basis of true religion. God is a Spirit, as to his nature; almighty, all-knowing, and everywhere present; searching the hearts and trying the thoughts of men. As to his moral attributes, it is said, "God is love," and "God is light;" by which we are to understand, that he is both benevolent and holy. Yes; so holy, that the very heavens are unclean before him. He is also so inflexibly just, as to be compelled, by the infinite per-

fection of his nature, to reveal his wrath against all ungodliness and unrighteousness of men; and, at the same time, he is a God who cannot lie, but will fulfill every word of promise or threatening. Oh, my reader, dwell upon this view of the divine character; infinite hatred and opposition to sin; infinite purity, immutable justice, inviolable truth. Pause and ponder! Can you lift up your eyes, and bear the sight of this glorious God, when the cherubim veil their faces with their wings, as they stand before the great white throne, and say one to another, "Holy, holy, holy, is the Lord God Almighty!" When the prophet filled with terror, fell prostrate, exclaiming, "Woe is me, for I am undone, because I am a man of unclean lips!" Oh the deep depravity, the utter sinfulness of man before this holy God!

2. You must understand the *moral law.* You must know the *spirituality* of the law, by which I mean, that it demands the obedience of the mind and heart; and is made for the soul's innermost recesses, as well as for the actions of the life. God sees and searches the mind, and therefore demands the perfect obedience of the heart, and forbids its evil dispositions. By the law of God, as interpreted by Christ, even sinful anger is murder, and unchaste thoughts are adultery. The law demands from every human being sinless, perfect obedience, from the beginning to the end of life, in thought, word, and deed; it abates nothing of its demands, and makes no allowances for human weakness (Matt. 5:17-48; James 2:10, 11). The perfection of the law is a tremendous subject; it is an awful mirror for a sinful creature to look into.

You must also understand the *design* of the law; it is not given to save us, but to govern us and *condemn* us; to show us what sin is, and to condemn us for committing it (Rom. 3:20; Gal. 3:10). You can know nothing if you do not know the law. "Sin is the transgression of the law;" but how can you know sin if you do not know the law? Oh, inquirer, how many, how great are your transgressions, if every departure from this law, in feeling as well as in action, is a sin! Nor is this all; for to fall short of the law is sin, no less than to oppose it. Read what our Lord has said; "You shall love the Lord your God with all your heart, and with all your soul, and with all your mind; and you shall love your neighbor as yourself." Alarming representation! Have *you* thus loved God, and your neighbor? Confounding and overwhelming question! What a *state of sin* have you been living in! Your whole life has been sin, for you have *not* loved God; and not to love God, is all sins in one. Who can think of greater sin than not loving God? To love the world, to love trifles, to love even sin—and not to love God!

3. But this leads me to remark, that it is necessary you should understand the *evil of sin*. Men think little of sin—but does God? What turned Adam and Eve out of paradise? Sin! What drowned the old world in the flood? Sin! What destroyed God's own city, and scattered his chosen people as vagrants over the face of the earth? Sin! What brought disease, accidents, toil, care, war, pestilence, and famine into the world? Sin! What has converted the world into one great burying-place of its inhabitants? Sin! What lights the flames of hell? Sin! What crucified the Lord of life and glory? Sin! What then must sin be? Who but God, and what but his infinite mind, can conceive of its evil nature?

Did you ever consider that it was only *one* sin that brought death and all our woes into the world? Do you not tremble, then, at the thought that this evil is in *you*? Some will attempt to persuade you that sin is a trifle; that God does not take much account of it; that you need not give yourself much concern about it. But what says God himself, in his word, in his providence, in the torments of the damned, in the crucifixion of his Son? You have not only sin enough in yourself to *deserve* the bottomless pit, and to sink you to it, unless it be pardoned; but sin enough, if it could be divided and distributed to others, to doom multitudes to perdition.

4. But it is not enough to know your *actual sins*, you must also clearly understand your *original and inherent depravity of heart*. There is the sin of your nature, as well as the sin of your conduct. Our Lord has told us that "those things which proceed out of the mouth, come forth from the heart, and they defile the man; for out of the heart proceed evil thoughts, murders, adulteries, fornications, thefts, false witness, blasphemies" (Mat.15:18-19). The heart is the polluted fountain from whence all the muddy streams of evil conduct flow! The heart is the great storehouse of iniquity! Men sometimes make excuse for their evil deeds, by saying, that they have good hearts at bottom; this, however, is an awful mistake, for every man's heart, not excepting the most wicked, is really worse than his conduct.

Why do not men seek, serve, and love God? Because the carnal mind is enmity against him. Why do sinners go on in sin? Because they love sin in their hearts. This was not the original condition of man, for God created Adam in his own image; that is, in righteousness and true holiness; but, by disobeying God in eating the forbidden fruit, our first parent fell into a state of sin, and we, having descended from him, since the fall, inherit his corruption (Rom. 5:12-21). It is of vast consequence for you to know, that you are thus totally corrupt in your very nature, and through all your faculties; for without this knowledge you will be taken up with a mere outward reformation, to the neglect of an entire, inward renovation. If you saw a man, who had a bad and loathsome disease of the skin, merely applying outward lotions and fomentations, you would remind him, that the seat of the disorder was in his blood, and admonish him to purify that by medicine. You must first make the tree good, said our Lord, for good fruit cannot be borne by a bad tree. So your heart must be renewed, or you can never perform good works. You not only need the pardon of actual sin, but you need also the removal of original sin. You must have a new heart, a right spirit, or you cannot be saved. Read Psalm 51; 53; John 3:1-8; Gal. 5:19-25; Eph.. 4:17-24.

5. You must endeavor at once to gain clear and distinct notions of *the precise design of Christ's mediatorial office and work.* All will be confusion in your ideas, and unrelieved distress in your souls, if you do not understand this subject. It is not enough to know in a general way, that Christ died to save sinners. Did it ever occur to you to ask the questions—*Why* did God save sinners in this way? Why was it necessary for his Son to become incarnate, suffer and die upon the cross, for their salvation? Why was it not enough that they should repent and reform, in order to their being pardoned? What precise end was to be accomplished by the death of Christ?

I will show you this design *as it relates to God.* Is not God holy, and does he not abhor sin? Yes! with a perfect hatred! Is he not the righteous Governor of the universe, and has he not given a law, to which he demands perfect obedience; and has he not threatened death upon all who break this law? Certainly! Have not all men broken this law and incurred its penalty? Yes! Suppose, then, that upon the sinner's mere sorrow for his sinful life, that God were to receive him back to his favor— and suppose he was to do this in every case. Where would God's truth be—in threatening to follow sin with punishment; and how would his holiness or hatred of sin appear, or his justice in punishing it? Would it not seem a light thing to sin against God; would not the law be destroyed, and God's moral government be set aside? Could any government, human or Divine, exist with an indiscriminate dispensation of pardon to all offenders upon their sorrow for the offences they have committed?

But you say perhaps, What is to be done? Is not sorrow for the sins committed, all that the sinner has to offer? I reply—Is sorrow for sin all that God is bound to require or accept? Besides, it is not all that the sinner has to give—for he can also suffer the penalty. Convinced and anxious sinner, I put it to your own conscience and feelings, do you not begin to see the holiness of God and the evil of sin; and do you think you could ever be at rest, if you had nothing but your sorrow to offer? No, you have tried it. You have left off many sins, and begun many neglected duties; you have read, and prayed, and wept, and watched; but are you at peace? No you are as far from it as ever! Why? Because you know that God is true, and holy, and just, and yet you cannot see how he can be holy, true, and just, if your sins are forgiven upon your mere sorrow and reformation.

True; and your conscience will ever be as the sword of the cherubim, frightening and driving you back from God as long as you have nothing but tears, and prayers, and doings of your own to bring. Yes, there is a testimony to God's holiness and justice in your conscience. "For no flesh will be justified in His sight by the works of the law, for through the law comes the knowledge of sin. But now, apart from the law, God's righteousness has been revealed—attested by the Law and the Prophets—that is, God's righteousness through faith in Jesus Christ, to all who believe, since there is no distinction. For all have sinned and fall short of the glory of God. They are justified freely by His grace through the redemption that is in Christ Jesus. God presented Him as an atoning sacrifice through faith in His blood, to demonstrate His righteousness, because in His restraint God passed over the sins previously committed. He presented Him to demonstrate His righteousness at the present time, so that He would be righteous and declare righteous the one who has faith in Jesus." (Romans 3:20-26) "The Lord has laid upon him the iniquity of us all." "He died, the just for [in place of] the unjust, to bring us to God" (1 Peter 3:16).

So far as God is concerned, then, this is the precise design of Christ's death, not to render him merciful, for the gift of Christ is the fruit of Divine love; but that he might appear what he is, a holy God in hating sin, a righteous God in punishing it, and a merciful God at the same time in forgiving it. The death of Christ is intended to be a display of holy love; that is, the union of abhorrence to the sin—and compassion to the sinner; the union of a just regard to his own character, law, and government—and a merciful regard to the sinful and miserable children of men. Take an illustration—Zaleucus[1], king of the Locrians, had promulgated a law to his subjects, threatening anyone who should be guilty of the crime of adultery, with the loss of his eyes. His own son was the first convicted under the law. The 'kingly' and 'parental' character seemed to struggle for predominance—if the prince is freely pardoned, the law would be violated. If the son is punished and executed, how great a calamity would the father endure in the affliction of the son! What was to be done? The father determined that *he* would lose *one* of his eyes, and the son one of *his*. It was done. Here was punishment and pardon united. Atonement was made to the offended law, as effectually as if the son had lost both of his eyes. The *letter* of the law was not complied with, but the spirit of it was exceeded. The case is not adduced as a perfect parallel to the atonement of Christ, but simply as an illustration of its principles, as tending to show that atonement may be as effectually made by substitution, as by the suffering of the real offender.

Anxious sinner, dwell upon Christ—he is your hope, your joy, your life. Behold the Lamb of God bearing the sins of the world, and yours among the rest. Think of the dignity of the Sufferer, the extremity of his sufferings, and the consequences of his atoning sacrifice. Could the law ever be more honored than by the obedience of *such* a Person? Could justice be more

---

1   Greek lawgiver of Epizephyrian Locri, in Italy, said to have devised the first written Greek law code, the Locrian Code.

displayed even by the everlasting punishment of all the human race? Tremble not to approach God through Christ. He has made provision for the manifestation of his own glory—as well as for the salvation of your soul. God is upon a throne of grace—the blood of atonement has been shed and sprinkled; the hand of mercy holds forth the blessing of salvation—fix your eye upon Jesus the Mediator; rest all your hope upon his sacrifice; plead his atonement, and then life eternal is yours!

6. But you must also be instructed in the design of Christ's death *in reference to yourself.* This is immensely important; it is often but partially understood by the inquirer, amidst the throbbing solicitude of his spirit, and the first alarms of conscious guilt. With the avenger of blood pursuing him, he is apt to think of little else than safety from vengeance. But there is another enemy he has to fear besides hell, and that is sin! And could he be delivered from hell, without being delivered from sin, he would find no heaven!

When man was created, he was created holy—and consequently happy. He was not only placed in a paradise which was without sin—but he was blessed with a paradise within him. His perfect holiness was as much the Eden of his soul, as the garden which he tilled was the Eden of his bodily senses—it was in the inward paradise of a holy mind that he walked in communion with God. The 'fall' cast him out of this heaven upon earth—his understanding became darkened, his heart became corrupted, his will became perverted, his nature became earthly, sensual, and devilish.

Not only was his conscience laden with guilt, but, as a necessary consequence, his imagination was full of terror and dread of that holy God, whose voice and presence formerly imparted nothing but transport to his soul. He became afraid of God, and unfit for him. His whole soul became the seat of fleshly appetites and sinful passions.

In his former innocence he had loved God supremely. He had been united to God by a feeling of dependence and devotedness. But now he was cut off from both these feelings, and came under the domination of an absorbing and engrossing selfishness. Such is the sinful nature he has transmitted to all his posterity. They are not only guilty—but depraved; not only under the wrath of God—but robbed of His image; not only condemned by God—but alienated from Him.

True it is, that hell will be some place set apart for the wicked, where the justice of God will consign them to the misery which their sins have deserved. But what is that misery? An eternal abandonment of them to themselves, with all their vices in full maturity! Hell is not only the wrath of God suffered, but that wrath coupled with an eternal endurance of all the tyranny of sin! Hence, then, the design of the death of Christ is not only to deliver us from the penalty of sin, but also from the polluting consequences of sin.

Now the death of Christ is intended as a deliverance from the power of sin. "His name is Jesus, for he shall save his people *from* their sins;" not *in* them. "Who gave himself for us, that he might redeem us from all iniquity, and purify unto himself a peculiar people, zealous of good works." "Christ loved the church, and gave himself for it; that he might sanctify and cleanse it, with the washing of water by the word; that he might present it to himself a glorious church, not having spot, or wrinkle, or any such thing; but that it should be holy and without blemish" (Eph. 5:25-27). And hence it is said to be the profession of believers in their baptism, to be under obligation to a conformity to the ends and designs of Christ's death (Rom. 6:1-7).

Do then, my dear friends, take up at once right views of the design of the work of Christ. You are to look to him for *salvation*—but what *is* salvation? Not only pardon; not only absolution from punishment; not merely deliverance from the bottomless pit; these blessings are, I admit, a part, but they are only a part of it—salvation means the crucifixion of your flesh, with its affections and lusts; the mortification of your corrupt nature. The salvation which the gospel offers is not only a future deliverance from hell—but a present deliverance from sin; not only a rescue from the punishment of sin—but a restoration to not only to the favor of God, but also to his image. Christ died to raise you to the seat of Adam before his fall, that is, to a holy state. The end of all God's dealings in a way of mercy to the sinner, is to restore the dominion of holy principles in his nature. The whole manifestation of holy love in the gospel, is designed to change the stubborn, selfish, worldly, wicked heart of the fallen creature—into God's holy likeness; and thus by making him a partaker of the Divine nature, to fit him for communion with God.

Now let every anxious inquirer consider this; let him ask what it is he needs, as a fallen, sinful creature. Is it not the deliverance of his soul from the *power* of sin—as well as the *punishment* of sin? Is he not painfully conscious to himself, not only of wrath coming down upon him from God for his sins, but of a spring of misery within himself in the existence of those very sins? And is it not for this he should look to Christ? Could he be saved at all, if not saved from his body of flesh, his corrupt nature? And can anyone save him from this but Christ? Poor troubled tormented sinner, look to Christ! In him is all you need—the Son of God will be "made unto you wisdom, and righteousness, and sanctification, and redemption" (1 Cor. 1:30).

7. *Connected with this, is the momentous subject of the justification of a sinner in the sight of God.* You must soon be at the tribunal of God for judgment, and if you are not justified now, you must be condemned then. Yes, if you are not yet jus-

tified, which it is to be presumed you are not, you are now in a state of condemnation—"for he that believes not, is condemned already; the wrath of God abides on him." Everyone who has not yet received Christ is under the curse of the law; he is a dead man in law, a sinner doomed to die; condemned by God, condemned to eternal death. Well may you tremble at your situation; and like the man, who, after condemnation at the court of his country's justice, has been removed to await in his cell the execution of his sentence, ask the question, "How shall I escape?"

At this stage of your experience, then, it is infinitely desirable you should be clearly instructed in the nature of justification. It is a subject of immense consequence to the sinner, and is therefore frequently mentioned, and treated at great length in the Epistles to the Romans and Galatians. Attend to the meaning of the word. *Justification* is the opposite of *condemnation*, as is evident from the following passages, "He who *justifies* the wicked and he who *condemns* the righteous, Both of them alike are an abomination to the LORD" (Prov. 17:15) and "Who shall lay anything to the charge of God's elect? It is God who *justifies*. Who is he that *condemns*?" (Rom. 8:33, 34). Fix this simple idea in your mind, that justification is the opposite of condemnation, for things are sometimes easily and impressively learned by their contraries.

The justification of an innocent person is pronouncing him just, on the ground of his own conduct. But how can a *sinner*, who is confessedly *guilty* of innumerable transgressions, be justified? Now you will see at once that the term, in reference to *him*, is a little different, and signifies, not that he is righteous in *himself*, but is 'treated as if he had been, through the righteousness of Christ imputed to him'. "Justification," says His name is Jesus the Assembly's larger Catechism, "is an act of God's free grace unto sinners, in which he pardons all their sins, accepts and accounts them as righteous in his sight, not for anything wrought in them, or done by them, but only for the perfect obedience and full satisfaction of Christ, by God imputed to them, and received by faith alone." In justification, God acts as a judge, in absolving the sinner from punishment, and restoring him to all the privileges of a citizen of the heavenly community.

Justification means not merely pardon, but something more. Pardon would only restore the sinner to the state of Adam before he fell, when he was not yet entitled to the reward of obedience, which, indeed, he never obtained. Justification is 'pardon' connected with a 'title to eternal life'. Justification takes place but once; pardon may be frequently repeated. Justification is that great change which is made in the sinner's relation to God, when he is delivered from condemnation, and is brought, from being an enemy, to be a child. If a king were to save a condemned criminal, and immediately adopt him as a child, this would resemble justification. And his frequent forgiveness of his after offences, when standing in the relation of a son, would resemble God's fatherly love in forgiving the sins of his children. Justification, then, is God's act in taking off the sentence of a sinner's condemnation by the law, restoring him to his favor, and granting him a title to eternal life in heaven.

But how can a righteous God, who has respect for his holy law, justify a sinner? I answer, on the ground of Christ's righteousness. The law is thus honored, because justification proceeds on the ground of a righteousness which meets and satisfies its demands. This is what is meant by the imputed righteousness of Christ—that the sinner is accepted to the Divine favor out of regard to what Christ did and suffered on his behalf. This judicial act of God, in justifying the sinner, takes place when and as soon as he believes in Christ; because by that act of faith he is brought into union with the Savior, and becomes legally one with him, so as to receive the benefit of his mediatorial undertaking.

In connection with this, it may be well to show the nature of <u>sanctification,</u> and how these two blessings are related to each other. Sanctification signifies our being set apart from the love and service of sin and the world, to the love and service of God; it is our being made holy; and a saint, or a sanctified person, means a holy one. Justification is the result of Christ's work *for* us; sanctification is the Holy Spirit's work *in* us.

Conceive of a criminal in jail under sentence of death, and at the same time infected with a fatal disease. In order to his being saved, he must be both pardoned and cured. For if he is only pardoned, he will soon die of his disease. And if he is only cured, he will soon be executed. Such is the emblem of the sinner's case; by actual sin he is condemned to die, by inherent depravity he is infected with a spiritual disease. In justification he is pardoned; in sanctification he is cured; and the two blessings, although distinct, are always united, and are both necessary to salvation. Thus you see justification changes our relation to God; but sanctification changes our spiritual condition. And regeneration, or the new birth, means our first entrance upon a sanctified state.

Reader, diligently attend to these things; fix your mind upon them; labor to understand them! A knowledge of these two blessings, justification and sanctification—is a key to the whole Bible. Oh blessed, infinitely blessed state! to be delivered from the condemnation of our sins, and from their domineering and defiling power, this *is a present salvation.*

8. You should also be well instructed *in the nature and necessity of the work of the Holy Spirit,* in renewing and sanctifying the sinner's heart. It is an important lesson, and one that should be learned at the very beginning of your pious course, that the work of the Holy Spirit in the sinner, is as necessary to his salvation as the work of Christ *for* him. As we are all cor-

rupt by nature, in consequence of our descent from Adam since his fall, we grow up and remain without any true religion, until it is implanted in the heart by Divine grace. True holiness is something foreign to our corrupt nature; and the whole business of the gospel, from first to last, is carried on in the heart by the Spirit of God. There is not a truly holy thought, feeling, purpose, word, or action—but is the result of Divine influence upon the human mind.

Our regeneration, or new birth, is ascribed to the Spirit—hence it is said, "Except a man be born of water and of the Spirit, he cannot enter into the kingdom of God" (John 3:5). Our right knowledge of God's word is traced up to the Spirit; hence David prayed, "Open my eyes, that I may behold wondrous things out of your law" (Psa. 119:18). Paul also prayed for the illumination of the Spirit, on behalf of the Ephesians, 1:17, 18. Sanctification is entirely the work of the Spirit; see 2 Thess 2:13; 1 Pet. 1:2. Believers are said to "live in the Spirit," "to walk in the Spirit;" "to walk not after the flesh, but after the Spirit;" "to be led by the Spirit," "to mortify the deeds of the body by the Spirit," "to be sealed by the Spirit," "to have the Spirit bearing witness with their spirit that they are the children of God," "to enjoy the indwelling of the Spirit," and to "bring forth the fruits of the Spirit." Now from all these passages, and many more that might be quoted, it is evident that the work of genuine religion is, from first to last, carried on in the soul by the Holy Spirit. This is *his* department, so to speak, in the economy of our redemption. The Father is represented as originating the plan of salvation; the Son as executing it; the Spirit as applying it. But in order that your mind may not be perplexed, as is sometimes the case, by this doctrine, I will make one or two remarks on the subject of 'Divine influence'.

The design of the Spirit's influence is not to give new mental faculties, but a proper exercise of those we already possess. This great work is intended to create a new heart in the sinner, which means a new and holy disposition. Man by nature is so depraved that he cannot love God; that is, he is so desperately wicked, that he is not in a mind to love him, and never will be —until God changes his mind.

The work of the Holy Spirit upon the mind is very mysterious, and we ought not to spend time in endeavoring to comprehend it, nor to indulge in any speculations about it. Our Lord declares it to be a great mystery, where he says to Nicodemus, "The wind blows where it wills, and you hear the sound thereof, but cannot tell whence it comes, and where it goes—so is everyone who is born of the Spirit" (John 3:8). We see the effects of the wind, but we cannot account for the changes in the atmosphere; so it is in the conversion of a sinner. It will greatly arrest the progress of the inquirer to engage in any speculations about this, or any other mystery of Divine truth.

The work of the Spirit is not intended to supersede the use of our faculties, but to direct them aright. He does not work *without* us, but by us. He does not change, and convert, and sanctify us, by leaving us idle spectators of the work, but by engaging us in it. Hence the admonition of the apostle to the Philippians (Phil. 2:10-11)—"Work out your own salvation with fear and trembling, for it is God who works in you—both to will and to do of his good pleasure." The exhortation, you perceive, does not say, Since it is God that works, there is nothing for *you* to do, and you may therefore sit still. No! On the contrary, it is—you must work, for *God* works in you. God's working in us is a motive for our working. God's working is the breeze that wafts the ship along, but then the mariner must hoist his sail to catch it. God's working is the rain and sunshine that cause the seed to germinate and grow, but the farmer must plough and sow; for though the seed cannot grow without the influence of the heavens, so neither can it grow without the sowing of the farmer.

We cannot usually distinguish between the influence of the Spirit and the operations of our own faculties, nor is it necessary we should. We cannot tell where man ends, and God begins—nor ought we to trouble or perplex ourselves about the matter. Hence, instead of waiting for any sensible or ascertainable impulse of the Spirit, either before we begin to attend to religion at all, or before we engage in any particular exercise of it, we are immediately to engage all our faculties in it, in a spirit of entire dependence upon God. We are to fix our attention, to deliberate, to purpose, to resolve, to choose, just as we would in worldly matters. But we are to do all this with a feeling of reliance upon God, and in the very spirit of prayer.

It is our obvious duty to repent and to believe, and also to do this at once, and not only merely to *desire* to do it, or attempt to do it. But such is the depravity of our nature, that we never shall do it until God powerfully influences us. What we have to do, therefore, is immediately to obey the command to repent and believe; and to obey in the very language and feeling of that prayer, "Lord, help my unbelief." We must obey, not only believing that it is our duty to obey, but believing also that we shall be assisted to obey.

Hence the very essence of religion seems to be a spirit of vigorous exertion—blended with a spirit of unlimited dependence upon God in earnest prayer. An illustration may be borrowed from the case of the man with the withered arm, as recorded Matthew 12:10-13. Our Lord commanded him to stretch forth his hand, and he did not say, Lord, I cannot, it is dead; but, relying on His power who gave the injunction, and believing that the command implied a promise of help, if he were willing to receive it—he stretched it forth; that is, he willed to do it, and he was able. So it must be with the sinner; he is commanded to repent and believe, and he is not to say, I cannot for I am dead in sin; but he is to believe in the promised aid of grace, and to obey in a dependence upon Him, who works in men to will and to do.

CHAPTER FOUR

Repentance

"EXCEPT you repent, you shall all likewise perish!" Such was the dreadful and tremendous denunciation of our Lord, to those Jews who were at that time listening to his discourse. And except *you* repent, my reader, you will perish—perish body and soul in the bottomless pit, and perish everlastingly! There is a world of misery in that word, '*perish*'—it is as deep as hell, as broad as infinity, and as long as eternity! None can comprehend its meaning but lost souls—and they are ever discovering in it some new mystery of woe! This misery will be *yours*, unless *you* repent. Tremble at the thought, and pray to Him who was exalted "to give repentance" as well as "remission of sins," that he would confer this grace of repentance upon you.

But what is it to repent? It is more, much more than mere sorrow for sin—this is evident from what the apostle has remarked; "Godly sorrow works repentance to salvation not to be repented of" (2 Cor. 7:10). True sorrow for sin is a *part*, and *only* a part, of repentance; for the scripture just quoted evidently makes a distinction between them. If sorrow comprised the whole of repentance, then Cain, Ahab, and Judas all repented; and hell itself is full of penitents, for there is weeping and wailing and gnashing of teeth forever. Many, very many, grieve for their sins, who never repent of them. Men may grieve for the *consequences* of their sins, without mourning for the sins themselves.

The meaning of the word repent, generally used in the Scriptures, is a change of mind. Repentance, therefore, signifies *an entire change of a man's views, disposition, and conduct, with respect to sin.* It is equivalent in meaning to regeneration. The new birth means a change of heart, and repentance is that same change viewed in reference to sin. The author of repentance is the Holy Spirit; it is the effect of Divine grace working in the heart of man. The following things are included in true repentance.

1. *Conviction of sin.* True repentance includes conviction of sin. "When he [the Spirit] has come, said Christ, he shall convince the world of sin" (John 16:8). The true penitent has a clear view of his state before God as a guilty and depraved creature. All men *say* they are sinners—the true penitent *knows* it! They talk of it—he *feels* it! They have heard it from others, and taken it up as an opinion—he has learned it by the teaching of God, who has shown him the purity of the law, and the wickedness of his own conduct and heart, as opposed to the law. He has looked into that bright and faithful mirror, the Word of God, and has seen his exceeding sinfulness. He perceives that he has lived without God, for he has not loved, and served, and glorified him. This in his view is sin—his not loving and serving God. He may not have been profligate—but he has lived without God. And if he has been openly wicked, his lack of love to God has been the parent vice. He sees that all his worldly-mindedness, folly, and wickedness, have sprung from a depraved heart—a heart alienated from God. He formerly thought he was not quite as he ought to be—but now he perceives that he has been altogether what he ought not to be. He formerly he knew matters were not quite right—but he now

sees they were all wrong! He perceives clearly that he has been so great a sinner, that God would have been just had he cast him into hell. This is now his confession.

> *"Should sudden vengeance seize my breath,*
> *I must pronounce You just in death;*
> *And if my soul were sent to hell,*
> *Your righteous law approves it well."*

Can you subscribe to this, reader? If not, you are not yet convinced of sin as you must be. No man knows what sin is, and how sinful he is, who does not clearly see that he has deserved to be cast into "the lake which burns with fire and brimstone."

2. *Self-condemnation.* True repentance includes self-condemnation. As long as a person indulges a self-justifying spirit, and is disposed, if not to *defend* his sins, yet to excuse them— he is not truly penitent, he is not indeed convinced of sin. To frame excuses for sin, and to take refuge from the voice of accusation and the stings of conscience in rationalizing away sin —is the besetting infirmity of human nature, which first showed itself in our fallen parents, when the man threw the blame upon the woman, and the woman upon the serpent—and it has since continued to show itself in all their descendants. We very commonly hear those who have been recently led to see their sins, mitigating their guilt; one by pleading the peculiarity of his situation; another his bias or constitution; a third the strength of the temptation; a fourth imputes his actual sins to his original sin, and endeavors, on this ground, to lessen his sense of guilt. But there is no true repentance while this excuse-making frame of mind lasts. No, never until the sinner has cast aside all excuses, rejected all pleas of extenuation, and abandoned all desire of self-justification; never until he is brought to take the whole blame upon himself; never until he pronounces his own sentence of condemnation; never is he tru-

ly penitent until his mouth is stopped as to all excuses, and he is brought unfeignedly and contritely to exclaim, "Guilty! Guilty!"

Some such as the following, is now his sincere confession —"O injured Sovereign, O all-holy God, and all-righteous Judge, I can attempt to excuse myself no longer. I stand before you a convicted, self-condemned sinner. What has my life been but a course of rebellion against you? It is not this or that action alone, I have to lament. My whole soul has been deranged and depraved. All my thoughts, all my affections, all my desires, all my pursuits—have been alienated from you. I have not loved you, O God of holy love. O what a heart have I carried in my bosom—that could love the world, love my friends, love trifles, yes, love sin—but could not love you! Particular sins do not so much oppress me, as this awful, horrid state of my carnal mind at enmity against you. Oh what patience was it that you did not crush the poor feeble creature that had no virtue to love you, and no power to resist you! My whole life has been one continued state of sin; what seemed good was done from no good motive; for it was not done out of obedience or love to you, and with no intention to please or to glorify you. Once I thought as little of my sin, as I thought of the gracious and righteous God against whom it was committed—and even when the knowledge of sin began to glimmer on the dark horizon of my guilty soul, how perversely did I resist the light, and how deceitfully, wickedly, and presumptuously, did I attempt to stand up in judgment with you, and in proud self-confidence to plead my own cause. Oh with what lying excuses, and with what extenuations, did I make my wickedness more wicked, and tempt your vengeance, and seek to draw your thunderbolts upon my devoted head! Eternal thanks for your marvelous patience, and your matchless grace, in not only bearing with my provocations, but convincing me of my folly. Stripped of all my pleas, silent as to every excuse, I cast myself before you, uttering only that one confession,

'Guilty! Guilty!' and uttering only that one cry, 'Mercy! Mercy!'"

3. *Sorrow for sin.* True repentance includes sorrow for sin. If a man does not mourn for sin, he cannot repent of it. The apostle speaks of "godly sorrow," and the psalmist exemplifies it in the fifty-first Psalm. Awakened and anxious sinner, I commend to your especial attention that affecting and precious effusion of David's contrition. Read it often; read it upon your knees in your closet; read it as your own prayer; read it until your heart responds a sigh to every groan with which each verse is still vocal. With those melting strains of a broken heart sounding in your ears, review the history of your life, and the dark and winding course of your rebellion against God. Pause and ponder as you trace back your steps, in each scene of your transgression—and God's infinite patience to you. Dwell upon the length of your term of sin, and all the aggravations of that sin arising from religious advantages, pious friends, and a reproving conscience. Assail your hard heart with motives to contrition, fetched from every view of God's mercy and your own ingratitude; nor cease to smite the rock until the waters of penitence gush forth. Nor let your sorrow be *selfish*; mourn more for your sins as committed *against* God, than against yourself.

Turn again to the fifty-first psalm, and see how David felt —"Against you, *you only, have I sinned, and done this evil* in your sight." Wonderful language! What views of sin were then in his mind; and, oh! what views of God! He had seduced Bathsheba into the greatest sin a wife can commit; he had murdered her husband; and had thus committed two of the most enormous evils against the well-being of society! And yet so impressed was he with a sense of his sin as committed against God, that he could now think only upon this—"*Against you,* you holy, holy, holy Lord God, have I sinned. *Against you,* my Benefactor, who raised me from the sheepfold to be the governor of your people. Oh, *this* is the crimson hue of my offence; *this* is the sting of my remorse; this is the wormwood and the gall of the cup of bitterness I now drink. You are willing to forgive me, and the thought of your amazing mercy blackens my crime, and deepens my self abhorrence." *This* is *godly* sorrow; a grief for sin as sin, and as committed against so holy and gracious a God, and not merely a grief for the mischief we have done to ourselves. Godly sorrow grieves for those sins which God only knows; for those sins which it knows he will *forgive*, yes, which it is assured he *has* forgiven; and this is the test of genuine contrition. Do we mourn for sin as sin, or only for fear of punishment?

4. True repentance includes *hatred of sin, forsaking it*, and a *determination not to repeat it*. No man can truly repent of an act without a feeling of dislike to that act; the two cannot be separated, yes, they are the same thing. Reformation produced by penitence is repentance. A person stung by a serpent will not caress the reptile, while, with the tears of sorrow, he bathes the wounds which that viper has inflicted. No! he will destroy the viper, or flee from him, and will ever after be inspired with fresh terror and dislike of the whole serpent brood. The true penitent regards sin as the viper that has stung him, and will ever after hate it, dread it, and watch against it. Practices that before were delighted in, will be abhorred and shunned; and instead of trying how near he may come to them without committing them, or how many things he may do that are like them, without doing the *very* things; he will try how far he can retire from them, and how entirely he may avoid the very appearance of evil. Will the serpent-bitten man see how near he can approach the rattle-snake without being stung again? Or will he fondle like reptiles, even though they may be without venom? No! Observe how repentance wrought in the members of the Corinthian church—"For having sorrow in a godly way results in repentance that leads to salvation and leaves no regrets. But the sorrow of the world produces death. See what

great earnestness godly sorrow has produced in you! How ready you are to clear yourselves, how indignant, how alarmed, how full of longing and enthusiasm, how eager to seek justice!" (2 Cor. 7:11). Such is repentance.

But it is important to guard the inquirer against some per-plexities with which many are very apt to trouble themselves on this subject.

You are not to suppose that you do not repent, because *you have never been the subject of overwhelming terror and exces-sive grief.* People in the first stages of religious impression are sometimes cast down and discouraged, because they do not feel those agonizing and terrifying convictions, that some, whom they have heard or read of, have experienced. Others, again, are greatly troubled because they do not and cannot shed tears and utter groans, under a sense of sin, as some do. If they could either be wrought up to terror, or melted into weep-ing, they should then take some comfort, and have some hope, that their convictions were genuine. Now it is very probable that you, reader, have these fears, and are laboring under some mistakes as the ground of them.

It may be, that this longing after great terror or deeper grief *may spring from a wrong motive.* If you possessed these feelings, you would be comforted, and have hope, you think— yes, and thus by looking to your own feelings for comfort, make a Savior of your experience, instead of Christ, as I fear many do. "Oh!" say some, or if they do not say it, they feel it, "now I have had such deep convictions, and such meltings of heart, I think I may hope." But is not this putting their feelings in the place of the work of Christ? If you could endure for a while the torments of hell in your conscience, and shed all the tears of all the penitents in the world, *they* would not save you. And to take comfort and hope from these things will be resting on a sandy foundation.

But, perhaps, you think this deep experience would be a stronger ground of confidence to go to Christ. Is not his own word, then, a sufficient warrant? Do you need *any other* warrant, or can you have any other? Is not his invitation and promise enough? What can your feelings add to this? In some cases, there is pride at the bottom of this longing after terror and distress—the person who covets it wishes to be distinguished among Christians for his deep experience and great attainments. Or he may wish to have something of his own to dwell upon with pleasure, a something that shall embolden him in his approach to God; it is, in fact, a subtle species of self-righteousness, a looking to inward feelings, if not to good works—as something to depend upon, and to boast in.

This anxiety may arise also *from a partial and incorrect view of the nature of real religion.* True religion is not a matter of mere feeling and strong emotion—but a matter of judgment, conscience, and practical principle. You must recollect that the minds of men are variously constituted as regards susceptibility of emotion. Some people are possessed of far livelier feelings than others, and are far more easily moved; we see this in the common subjects of life as well as in religion. One man feels as *truly* the affection of love for his wife and children as another whose love is more vehement, though he may not fondle, caress, and talk of them so much—he may not even suffer those terrors of alarm when anything ails them, nor of frantic grief when they are taken from him. But he loves them so as to prefer them to all others, to labor for them, to make sacrifices for their comfort, and really to grieve when they are removed. His love and grief are as sincere and practical, though they are not boisterous, passionate, and noisy—his principle of attachment is as strong, if his passion is not so ardent.

Passion depends on constitutional temperament, but principle does not. Mere emotion, therefore, whether in religion or other matters, is no test of the genuineness of affection. Do not then, my reader, be troubled at this matter; your religion is not to be tried by the number of tears you shed, or the degree of terror you feel, or the measure of excitement to which you are wrought up. There may be much of all this emotion, where there is not true repentance; and there may be little of it, where there is true repentance.

Are you clearly instructed in the knowledge of God's holy nature and perfect law, so as distinctly to perceive, and really to feel, and frankly to confess, your numberless sins of conduct and deep depravity of heart? Do you truly admit your just desert of that curse which your sins have brought upon you? Do you cast away all excuses, and take the whole blame of your sins upon yourself? Do you really mourn for your sins, although you may shed few tears or utter few broken groans? Do you confess your sins to God without reserve, as well as without excuse? Do you truly hate sin, and abhor yourself on account of sin? Do you feel a repugnance to sin, a watchfulness against it, a dread of it in the least offences? Are you possessed of a new and growing tenderness of conscience with respect to sin? Then you are partakers of true repentance, although you may not be the subjects of those violent emotions, either of terror or of grief, which some have experienced.

I do not for a moment mean to throw suspicion upon the experience of those who have been called to pass through a state of conviction, which, on account of its terrific alarms and unutterable anguish, may be called the valley of the shadow of death. By no means. God has led some of his people, not only hard by the clouds and blackness, the thunders and earthquakes, the trumpet and awful words of Sinai—but almost by the very brink of the burning pit, within sight of its flames, and within sound of its wailings! But let no man covet such a road to glory; let no man think he has mistaken the road, because he has not witnessed these dreadful scenes in his way. All must pass by both mount Sinai and mount Calvary in the way to heaven—but the view of each of them is not so clear or so impressive to some, as it is to others.

CHAPTER FIVE

Faith

SUPPOSE a number of the subjects of a wise and good king were, without any just cause, to rebel against him, and take up arms to dethrone him, they would by that act forfeit their lives. But suppose that the sovereign, in clemency, is disposed to pardon them, and for that purpose, sends out a proclamation, declaring that all those who, before a fixed time, would come to him, lay down their arms, confess their offence, and sue for mercy, should be spared, and restored to all their privileges as citizens; but that all who would be found under arms, and did not come and cast themselves upon the mercy of their sovereign, should be put to death. What, in this case, is the state of mind and act required in those who would be saved? Faith. They must believe the proclamation to have been issued by the monarch, and that he will really fulfill his word; they must not only believe the edict itself, but they must confide in *the monarch*; this is faith *in him*. What is their warrant or encouragement to go to him? His proclamation of mercy, and that alone; and not any convictions or desires of their own. If any of the rebels were desirous of returning, he would not say, "I am greatly encouraged and truly warranted to go and expect forgiveness, because I am very anxious to be forgiven;"

for his desire of pardon of itself, is no warrant to expect it; but he would say, "My sovereign has *bade* me return, and *promised* me pardon—I have his word, and I can trust him—I will go, therefore, and confidently expect mercy." He goes, and although he knows that he has forfeited his life and deserved death, and brought himself under condemnation; yet he is assured he shall be spared, because the King has promised it, and he trusts in his veracity. This is faith. Does his faith merit forgiveness? No, but it insures it. Can the man boast that his works have saved him? No—he is saved by grace, through faith.

But suppose when he heard the proclamation of mercy, he was merely convinced of his sin, and in some measure sorry for it, and desired forgiveness, *but did not go to his sovereig*n; suppose he were to say to himself, "I am afraid to go; the prince is powerful, being surrounded by his guards who could destroy me in a moment, and I have been such a ringleader in the rebellion that I cannot hope for mercy, although I long for it, and would do anything to obtain it." The time of mercy expires; the man is taken with weapons in his hands; and he is put to death. Does he deserve to die? Yes, twice over, first for his rebellion, and secondly for his unbelief. His lack of faith, not his rebellion, was the actual cause of his death. His sin would have been pardoned, had he believed. His convictions, his sorrow, his tears, his desire after pardon, could not save him—he had insulted his sovereign afresh, by doubting his truthfulness, and disobeying his command.

Awakened sinner, take heed that this is not your case. It is the case of many. They are rebels against God, they are guilty of innumerable sins. "God so loved the world, that he gave his only begotten Son, that whoever believes in him should not perish, but have everlasting life." "It is a faithful saying, and worthy of all acceptance, that Christ Jesus came into the world to save sinners." Thus runs the proclamation of mercy—"Repent of sin, believe in Christ, expect salvation." Many *do* believe, and are saved—but others, and they are multitudes, *get no further than conviction*; they know they are sinners, they desire pardon, and seem even willing to forsake some of their sins; but they do not believe in Christ, they do not return to God by faith in his Son, indulging a confident hope of forgiveness—they are afraid to go, saying their sins are too great to be forgiven; or they are contented to remain in a state of conviction; or before they have trusted in Christ, and experienced a real change of heart through faith, some earthly object or other draws off their attention from the Savior, and they sink into a state of carelessness, and gradually go back again into the world.

You are never safe, reader, until you have faith. Whatever may have been your tears, convictions, prayers, or exercises of mind, you are under the sentence of the law, and exposed to the wrath of God until you believe. If death come upon you before you have faith, you will as certainly and as deservedly perish, as the rebel, who, though he had expressed his sorrow for his treason, had not come in and cast down his weapons, and accepted the royal mercy. You are within the flood-mark of Divine vengeance until you have confided your soul to Christ. Can we be saved if we are not justified? No! But we are "justified by *faith*, and have peace with God" (Rom. 5:1). Can we be saved unless we are the children of God? No! But we are "all the children of God by *faith* in Christ Jesus" (Gal. 3:26). Can we be saved without sanctification? No! Then "our hearts are purified by *faith*."

But the jailor at Philippi asked, with fear and trembling, the question, "What shall I do to be saved?" Paul replied, "<u>Believe</u> *on the Lord Jesus Christ, and you shall be saved*" (Acts 16:31). When our Lord sent out his disciples, he said unto them, "Go into all the world, and preach the gospel to every creature—he who <u>believes</u> and is baptized shall be saved, but he who *believes not shall be damned*" (Mark 16:15,16). It is also said in another place, "He who believes on him is not condemned; *but he who believes not, is condemned already, because he has not believed* on the name of the only begotten Son of God. He who believes on the Son has everlasting life; he who believes not the Son, shall not see life, but the wrath of God abides on him" (John 3:15,16). "He who believes on the Son of God has the witness in himself; he *who believes not God, has made him a liar; because he believes not the record that God gave of his Son*" (John 5:10). See then the importance, the tremendous importance, of faith in Christ. It is the hinge on which salvation turns; it is that, without which all knowledge, and all impressions, and all convictions, and all duties, will leave us short of heaven at last. Fix it deeply in your mind, therefore, that faith is the saving grace; or, in other words, that it is the state of mind with which salvation is connected; being brought into this state, you would be saved though you died the next hour; and without it you would not be saved, even had you been for years under the deepest concern for your soul.

But you will probably wish to know a little more about this transcendently important state of mind; and I shall, therefore, set before you,

1. *What you are to believe.* Faith, in general, means a *belief of whatever* God has testified in his word; but *faith in Christ* means the belief of what the Scripture says of him; of his person, offices, and work. You are to believe that he is "the Son of God;" "God manifest in the flesh;" God-man, Mediator —for how can a mere creature be your Savior? In faith you commit your soul to the Lord Jesus. What! into the hands of a mere creature? The Divinity of Christ is thus not merely an article of faith, but enters also into the foundation of hope. You are required to believe in the doctrine of atonement; that Christ satisfied Divine justice for human guilt, having been a propiti-

ation for our sins; and that now his sacrifice and righteousness are the only ground or foundation on which a sinner can be accepted and acquitted before God. You are to believe that all, however previously guilty and unworthy, are welcome to God for salvation, without any exception, or any difficulty whatever. You are to believe that God really loves the world, and is truly willing and waiting to save the chief of sinners, and that he therefore is benevolent to *you*. And thus, instead of dwelling in the idea of a mere general or universal love, you are to bring the matter home to yourself, and to believe that God has goodwill towards you, has given Christ to die for *you*; that you are a part of the world which God loved, and for which Christ died, and you are not to lose yourself in the crowd. You are not to consider the scheme of redemption for anybody, or for everybody, but yourself; but you are to give the whole an individual bearing upon yourself. You are to say, "God is well disposed towards *me*; Christ is given for *me*; died for *me* as well as for others—I am invited; I shall be saved if I trust in Christ; and I am as welcome as anyone to Christ."

Faith is not a belief in your own personal religion, that is the assurance of hope; but it is a belief that God loves sinners, and that Christ died for sinners, and for you among the rest. It is not a belief that you are a real Christian, but that Christ is willing to give you all the blessings included in that term. It is the belief of something out of yourself, but still of something concerning yourself. The object of faith is the work of Christ for you—not the work of the Spirit in you. It is of great consequence you should attend to this, because many are apt to confound these things. If I promise a man alms, and he really believes what I say, and expects relief, I, in the act of promising him, am the object of his faith, and not the state of his own mind in the act of believing. If, therefore, you would have faith, or, possessing it, would have it strengthened, you must fix and keep your eye on the testimony of Christ, which you find in the gospel.

2. *I will now show you 'how' you are to believe.* But is this necessary? There is no mystery in faith when we speak of believing a fellow-creature. When the rebel is required to believe in the proclamation of mercy sent out by his sovereign, and to come and sue for pardon, or when the beggar is required to believe in the promise of a benefactor who has promised him relief, does it enter into his mind to ask *how* he is to believe? What, in each of these cases, does faith mean? A belief that the promise has been made, and a confidence in the person who made it that he will fulfill his word.

Behold, then, the whole mystery there is in faith! It is a belief that Christ really died for sinners; that all who depend upon him alone shall be saved; and a trust in him for salvation. Yes, it is, if we may substitute another word as explanatory of faith, 'trust' in *Christ*. Faith, and confidence in Christ, are the same thing. "I know whom I have believed," says the apostle, "and am persuaded he is able to keep that which I have committed to him." Believing, being persuaded, and the act of committing, are the same act; they all mean faith. It is to rest upon the word and work of Christ for salvation; to depend upon his atonement and righteousness, and upon nothing else, for acceptance with God; and *really to expect salvation*, because he has promised it. If there is no expectation, there is no faith; for faith in a man's promise necessarily implies expectation of its fulfillment. This, then, is faith; looking for or expecting salvation for the sake of Christ's work alone, and because God has promised it.

If you want another illustration, take the case of the serpent-bitten Israelites (Num. 21:4-9, John 3:14). The people who were stung were commanded to look on the brazen serpent. Those who really believed the promise, that such an act would be followed with healing, went out and looked at the appointed means of relief—their looking was their believing; and what did that look imply? Expectation. Those who did not look did not expect healing, and those who did look expected relief. If, therefore, you are not brought to expect salvation, you do not believe; for as soon as you really believed you would indulge the expectation of salvation. "Faith is the substance [or confident expectation] of things hoped for." Faith being the expectation of salvation for Christ's sake alone, and because he has promised it, it may be said to be weak or strong in proportion as our expectation is more or less confident, and free from doubt and fears.

3. *But 'when' is a sinner to believe?* Strange question! And yet one that it is necessary to answer, because it is sometimes asked. Suppose, when you promised alms to a poor starving beggar, or forgiveness to a person that had injured you—he were to ask, "*When* am I to believe your promise?" Would you not feel some surprise at the question? The very nature of the case suggests the propriety and necessity of immediate faith. Your veracity is as great at that moment as it ever will be, and therefore demands instant confidence. Suppose the beggar were to say, "I do not yet sufficiently feel my poverty, to believe you *now*; but when I am more pinched with hunger, I will take you at your word and come." Would not this be exceedingly preposterous? And yet this is the very conduct of many people in reference to Christ, and faith in him for salvation. They know that trust in him alone is necessary to salvation; that they must at *length* come to him; but they seem to regard it rather as an exercise or state of mind, to which they are to be brought at some future time, and by some means they know not how, than as a duty to be *immediately* performed. Their inward feeling is, a hope that they shall have faith some time or other, without ever imagining that they are required, *at once* and without delay, to commit their soul to Christ.

Reader, reflect upon this matter, this necessity of instantly believing. Are you now a sinner? You know you are. Can you do anything now or hereafter to save yourself? You know you cannot. Is Christ *now* a Savior, able and willing to save you *now*? You know he is. Will he be more able or willing to save you a month or a year hence, than he is at this moment? Certainly not. Does he say, "Come unto me, *not now, but at some future time;* believe me, but not yet; trust in me after a while?" You know he does not. Every invitation, every promise, every encouragement, relates to the present moment. The words of Scripture are, "Today if you will hear his voice, harden not your hearts. Now is the accepted time, now is the day of salvation. Come, for all things are ready. He is waiting to be gracious."

What prevents you. Why should you not *now*, as you read this, believe in Christ? What, except your own unwillingness, hinders you from this moment trusting in the Lord Jesus for salvation? What, *now?* you say, still startled at the idea of instantly taking to your anxious bosom the sweet and soothing hope of salvation. "*Why not now?*" I ask. "Would God," you are ready to say, "I could; for I have no peace of mind! I feel that I am a sinner, and yet am distressed, at times, that I do not feel this enough. I am agitated and perplexed, for I have no reason to hope my sins are forgiven. I cannot approach God as a reconciled Father; on the contrary, I am afraid of him, and fear, if I were to die, I should not meet him in peace."

Permit me here to remind you, that you never *can* be at peace until you have faith—peace is the fruit, and the *first fruit* of faith. Observe what the apostle has said—"In whom, though now you see him not, yet *believing*, you rejoice with joy unspeakable and full of glory" (1 Pet. 1:8). It is said of the Philippian jailer, "he rejoiced, *believing* in God" (Acts 21:34). You never can, until you believe in Christ, have settled peace of mind, except it be a false peace; you are seeking it in various ways, and occasionally obtain a short pause in your solicitude, by prayer, by hearing sermons, by dwelling on what you suppose are evidences of your conversion, by fully purposing to leave off your sins, and to serve God more entirely. But notwithstanding all this, you are not in possession of settled comfort. Your joy is more like an occasional flash from a candle in a dark night, than a steady sunshine—so that sometimes you are ready to give up religion altogether, and turn back again to the world; for you seem to be as far from comfort as ever. But stop and ask this question, "Am I seeking peace in the right way? Have I ever yet really, fully, and entirely believed in Christ? Have I truly committed my soul to him, and expected salvation according to his promise?" No! for if you had, you would not be in your present state of agitation.

What is to give peace to a sinner feeling the burden of guilt upon his conscience? What is to relieve him from his distress? Nothing but faith *in Christ*; not the faith itself, but the *object* which faith looks at, which is Christ. Many are saying, "If I did but *know* that I had faith, or if I could feel my faith stronger, I could then rejoice." But this is seeking peace in faith itself, instead of seeking it by faith in Christ. Faith is not our Savior, but only the eye that looks to him, the foot that goes to him, the hand that receives him. Take an illustration— Imagine that when you were afflicted with some dangerous disease, and anxious for recovery; in the midst of your solicitude, and after trying all kinds of remedies without effect, a physician came in, and said, "I have brought you an infallible cure for your illness; it has cured thousands, and will most certainly cure *you*." What would be the effect of this communication upon you? Just according to the state of your mind in reference to the report which the physician gives of his medicine. If your concern about recovery, and your fear of not obtaining a cure, were greater than your faith, you would gain no peace; the lack of confidence in the medicine would keep you in deep solicitude.

But suppose you were to believe the statement of your medical friend, and had full confidence in the remedy, what then would be the effect of the report? You would *immediately* rejoice; you would not wait until you had taken the medicine, and until you felt yourself cured, before your solicitude was relieved; no, but as soon as you believed in the efficacy of the remedy, you would say, "Joyful news! I am to be healed and restored to health." Now what in that case would relieve you from your solicitude, and give you comfort? The statement of your friend, or, in other words, faith in that statement. The good news of a coming cure, believed by you, would make you glad. It would not be the act of believing that you would rejoice in, but the statement believed. You would immediately take the medicine; and when you experienced its healing influence, you would rejoice still more. Your joy in this case would be of two kinds—the first *the joy of faith*, in the assurance that you would be cured; the second *the joy of experience*, in finding that you were cured.

Apply this to the case of a sinner who feels his miserable condition under the power and guilt of sin. In his concern he tries various methods to obtain relief; he leaves off sin, and tries to be good; but a sense of unpardoned sin still lies upon his heart, and he is far off from settled comfort. In this situation, Christ, the physician of souls, comes to him in the message of the gospel, and says, "My blood *cleanses* from all sin, and my Spirit can renew and sanctify the hardest and most polluted heart; look to me, and you shall be saved!" What is the duty of the sinner in this case? Immediately, fully, and at once, to believe, and as the evidence and necessary fruit of his faith, to rejoice. If he really does believe, he *will rejoice*; and if he does not rejoice, it is because he does not believe. He is not to wait until he *is* saved, before he takes comfort; but he is to take comfort, in the first place, in believing that there is a Savior, and that he may be saved. He is not to wait for his comfort until he feels that he is justified, renewed, and sanctified; for how can he come to this state unless he believes? His first comfort must be the joy of faith; and this he must take to himself at once; the joy of experience comes afterward. He must first rejoice in the *promise* of spiritual healing, and then afterwards he will rejoice in the sense of healing.

When the Jews, who were pricked to the heart by Peter's sermon, cried out in agony, "What shall we do?" he replied, "Repent, and be baptized everyone of you in the name of Jesus Christ, for the remission of sins—then those who gladly received the word were baptized" (Acts 2:37-41). They gladly received the word, that is, they believed the promise and were made glad. There was immediate faith producing instant joy— they did not wait until they felt they were saved, but rejoiced at once. Now observe another case—Paul, in one of his epistles, says, "Our rejoicing is this, that in simplicity and godly sincerity, not with fleshly wisdom, but by the grace of God, we have lived our lives in the world" (2 Cor. 1:12). Here is the joy of experience. It is the peace of *believing*, that the inquirer has to do with. And is it not cause enough of delight that God has loved the world, and you, as a part of the world, so as to give his Son for your salvation; that you are invited; and that Christ is able and willing to save you? But still you cling to the idea, if you could be sure you believed, you would be comforted; if you had evidence of faith, you would take peace. Then it would be those evidences that would comfort you, and not the work of Christ.

It is also of importance that you should clearly understand, that you are never in a state of faith, if you are not brought to some degree of comfort; if you still feel the load of guilt upon your conscience, and all its tormenting fears in your mind; if you are still anxiously asking the question, "What shall I do to be saved?" If you are still afraid of God, if you still are without any hope of forgiveness, you do not believe; for genuine faith, even though it were not full assurance, would in some measure relieve you from this concern. It is very common for people to say they believe, and yet have no comfort; and then they are asking, "Why am I not at peace?" Because you do not really believe in Christ; you are deceiving yourself. It is faith, genuine faith, you need—you have not yet really trusted in Christ; you have not believed the glad tidings of salvation; for can any man believe glad tidings concerning himself, and yet not be made glad by them? Believe then, believe truly, believe now— and enter into peace.

CHAPTER SIX

Mistakes

Into Which Inquirers are Apt to Fall

IN an affair of such tremendous consequence as the salvation of the soul, it is important that every error of any importance into which inquirers are in danger of falling, should be clearly pointed out to them. Satan is called the father of lies, and when his delusive influence is added to the natural deceitfulness of the human heart, the danger of mistake in this matter is great indeed. Our caution against errors should, of course, be in proportion to the importance of the consequences they draw after them. Oh, how awful is the idea of committing a fundamental error in spiritual matters, and persevering in that error until death! We shall then have eternity to deplore it—but never have a moment to correct it! Oh how dreadful to die—and find ourselves mistaken as to our character and destiny! But even where the error is not of so serious a nature, it may still be the source of much disquietude.

1. The first error which inquirers are in danger of committing, (and it is both a very common and a very dreadful one,) is, *to mistake knowledge, impressions, and partial reformation*

—*for genuine conversion.* In this day when evangelical preaching and religious instruction are so abundant, where there is no persecution to test men's sincerity, and even much credit attaching to a profession of religion, there is most imminent danger of self-delusion. The preaching of the present day is of an exciting and impressive character, which, added to the knowledge acquired from a religious education, is very likely to produce a state of feeling that may be mistaken for conversion. Ignorant friends, concerned parents, and even injudicious ministers, who are too eager to swell the number of their members, upon perceiving a little impression of mind, and a little alteration of conduct—may express a favorable opinion of their conversion, flatter them into a belief that they are safe, and engage them too hastily to make a public profession of religion and receive the Lord's supper; while perhaps, the great change has never been wrought in them. And thus their souls are in all probability, sealed up in delusion to eternal perdition! Nothing can now awaken them; for although their impressions die away, and they become almost as careless, as worldly, as sinful as ever; yet they have taken up a profession of religion, have been led to believe they are Christians, and therefore repress every rising fear, and stifle every incipient alarm. Fatal case! And it is the case of multitudes!

It may be worth while to set before you how far people may go, and not be really converted. They may have many and deep religious impressions, many and strong convictions; they may have much knowledge of their sinful state, and a heavy and burdensome sense of their guilt; they may look back upon their past lives and conduct with much remorse; they may be sorry for their sins; and may desire to be saved from the consequences of them, being much alarmed at the prospect of the torments of hell. Was not Judas convinced of sin, and did not he weep bitterly and confess his sin, and was not he filled with remorse? Was not Cain convinced of sin? I have known many people, who at one time appeared to be more deeply impressed with a sense of sin, and to have stronger convictions and re-morse, than many who were truly converted—and yet they went back again to the world and sin.

Nor is a detestation of sin always a true sign of conver-sion. Hazael, before he was king of Syria, detested the crimes which he afterwards perpetrated in the fullness of his pride and power. Unconverted people may even wish to be delivered from the fetters of those corrupt lusts, which have long held them fast; for there are few notorious sinners, who do not fre-quently hate their sins, and wish and purpose to reform. Yes, people may sometimes desire to be delivered from all sin; at least they may desire it in a certain way, because they think that it is necessary in order to be saved from hell.

And as conviction of sin may exist without conversion, so may religious joy. "The stony ground hearers heard the word, and with joy received it,"[2] and yet they had "no root in them-selves, and endured only for a while." The Galatians had great blessedness at one time, which the apostle was afraid had come to nothing[3]. Multitudes rejoiced in Christ when he made his entrance into Jerusalem, who afterwards became his ene-mies. A person may admire the people of God, and covet to be of their number, as Balaam did, and yet not really belong to them. Many take great pleasure in hearing sermons, and going to prayer-meetings, and singing hymns, and frequenting mis-sionary and other public meetings, who are not truly born of the Spirit. So also do many people leave off sinful actions, and give up many wicked practices, and seem to be quite altered for a time, and yet, by their subsequent history, show that they are not converted.

There may be considerable zeal for the outward concerns of religion, as we see in Jehu, without any right state of mind

2   Mat. 13:20
3   Gal. 4:15

towards God. Many have had great confidence of the reality of their conversion; they have had dreams, impressions, and an inward witness, as they suppose—and yet too plainly proved, by their after-conduct, that they were under an awful delusion. But it would be almost endless to point out the various ways in which men deceive themselves, as to their state. Millions who have been somewhat, yes, much concerned about religion, have never been born again of the Spirit. Perhaps as many are lost by self-deception, as by any other means. Hell resounds with the groans and lamentations of souls which perished through the power of deceived hearts!

Do, do examine yourselves. Exercise godly jealousy over your own state. Never forget that nothing short of *the new birth* will save you. "Except a man be born of water and of the Spirit, he cannot enter into the kingdom of God" (John 3:5) "Therefore if anyone is in Christ, he is *a new creation. The old things have passed away. Behold, all things have become new*" (2Cor. 5:7). Our very nature must be changed, entirely changed. We must be renewed in the spirit of our mind. There must be a superhuman, a Divine, a total alteration of disposition. Our views and tastes, pains and pleasures, hopes and fears, desires and pursuits, must be changed. We must be brought to love God supremely, for his holiness and justice, as well as for his mercy and love in Christ; to delight in him for his transcendent glory, as well as for his rich grace. We must have a perception of the beauties of holiness, and love Divine things for their own excellence. We must mourn for sin, and hate it for its own evil nature, as well as its dreadful punishment. We must feel delight in the salvation of Christ, not only because it delivers us from hell, but makes us like God, and all this in a way that honors and glorifies Jehovah. We must be made partakers of true humility and universal love, and feel ourselves brought to be of one mind with God, in willing and delighting in the happiness of others. We must be brought to feel an identity of heart with God's cause, and to regard it as our honor and happiness to do anything to promote the glory of Christ in the salvation of sinners. We must feel a longing desire, a hungering and thirsting after holiness, as well as come to a determination to put away all sins, however gainful or pleasant. We must have a tender conscience, that shrinks from and watches against little sins, secret faults, and sins of neglect and omission, as well as great and scandalous offences. We must love the people of God, for God's sake, because they belong to him and are like him. We must practise the self-denying duty of mortification of sin, as well as engage in the pleasing exercises of religion.

This is to be born again—and it is no mere transient impression upon the imagination, but it is a permanent renewal of the disposition; it is not an occasional impulse, but an abiding character. The subject of it may not be violently agitated—but he is lastingly altered. His passions may not be powerfully moved—but his principles, tastes, and pursuits are engaged on the side of true holiness. He is now a spiritual man, whereas before he was a carnal one, and all things are now spiritually discerned by him. Nothing short of this entire change of heart, this complete renovation of the nature, must satisfy you; for nothing less than such a view of Christ in his glorious mediatorial character, and such a dependence by faith upon his blood and righteousness for salvation, as changes the whole heart, and temper, and conduct, throws the world as it were into the background, and makes glory hereafter, and holiness now, the supreme concern, is saving religion.

2. *Inquirers are often in error on the subject of their immediate obligation to believe, and go to Christ; and are waiting, as they say, for a day of power at the pool of ordinances.* They are seeking and praying, but they have no idea that it is their *present* duty, without waiting another hour, to give themselves to Christ. They are expecting some sensible impression or impulse upon their mind, to make known to them when it is

their duty to believe, and also *enable* them to believe. They suppose it will at some time be made clear to them, as it was to the cripples by the troubling of the waters, that they are no longer to wait, but immediately to descend into the pool of salvation.

Now this is a most grievous and injurious error, and keeps many minds for a long period in great distress, and actually prevents some from coming to Christ at all. I must first tell you, that it is an utter perversion of Scripture, to consider the pool of Bethesda as an emblem of the healing of sinners by the work of Christ; and the situation of the diseased people waiting for the healing visit of the angel, as descriptive of the duty of sinners to wait for some *impulse* or power from above, before they believe. The fact was related merely to show the power and glory of Christ in working a miraculous cure. Where in all the New Testament are sinners told to wait until some future time before they believe? Where is it said, "Believe, but not now; hope, but not now; wait for some power or impulse to enable you to believe?" On the contrary, is it not said, "Today if you will hear his voice, harden not your hearts; *now* is the accepted time, now is the day of salvation?"

Is not God willing to pardon you this moment; Christ willing to save you this moment; the Spirit waiting to renew and sanctify you this moment? Are not all the promises true now, all the blessings of salvation ready and waiting for your acceptance now? What then are you waiting for, or why should you wait at all? Could a voice from heaven, or any impulse in your hearts, make it more certain than the word of God makes it, that Christ is willing to save you? Look steadily at this promise, "Come unto me, all you who labor and are heavy laden, and I will give you rest." Is that the language of Christ? Yes! Is it true? Yes! Does it say anything about waiting for an impulse? No! What then are you hesitating about? It is as true this moment as it ever will or can be; and if you wait for anything else but the word of Christ, you will spend all your time in waiting, and die deceived at last! True, you need the influence of the Spirit, to assist you to believe, but that influence is always as ready as the benefit of the work of Christ.

But, say others, *"We are waiting to be more deeply convinced of sin."* Are you convinced that you are under the condemnation of the law; such a sinner as to be totally depraved in your nature, as well as guilty of innumerable actual sins, and deserving of hell? Is this clear to your judgment, and really felt by your conscience; then what are you waiting for? If you say, for more sorrow of heart, more pungent convictions, I would ask again—how deep do you suppose your convictions must be, before you believe in Christ, and hope for mercy? Can you fix on any standard on this subject? Besides, do you suppose that if your convictions were ten times as deep as they now are, these feelings of yours would be your warrant to go to Christ, or render you more welcome to him, or be in any measure your ground of hope? Are you not wishing for deep convictions, to take comfort in *them*—instead of Christ? Has Christ anywhere said, he will not receive you until your convictions have attained a certain depth? The question is—Are you *really* convinced? The question is not—How *deeply* are you convinced? And then, as to godly sorrow, this will be promoted by faith. "They shall look upon me whom they have pierced, and mourn," says the Lord Jesus, concerning the Jews (Zech. 12:10). The belief of God's love to us in Christ, and the sweet hope of his mercy, will melt the heart to tenderness.

I wish you to dwell upon this. It is the hope, the sense of God's love, that warms and thaws the cold and frozen heart of man. As you gaze upon a crucified Redeemer by faith—as you hear God say, "I, even I, am he who blots out your sins by the blood of my Son; I will forgive you all, notwithstanding your rebellion, and your too great lukewarmness"—your soul will dissolve in ingenuous grief and love. In keeping back from

Christ, in waiting for deeper emotions before you come to him, you are defeating your own purpose. The more and sooner you hope in Christ, the more and sooner will you mourn for sin. Every fresh view you take of his cross, when you are indulging an expectation of mercy, will deepen your emotions of sorrow, and your convictions of the evil of sin. All the sensibilities of your heart will be moved by the amazing spectacle; and that very scene which conveys to your soul the sense of pardon, will convey also a sense of the bitterness of your transgression. Wait no longer then, believe, believe *now*! Commit your soul at once to the Savior, and rejoice in hope of salvation.

Others are waiting for more holiness, for some preparatory process, before they rest upon Christ for eternal life. A preparatory process indeed there is, and must be carried on in the heart before the sinner will go to Christ. But what is that process? Nothing which is to prevent his soul, for a moment, when he is anxious about salvation, from depending upon Christ. It is the work of the Holy Spirit giving him a sense of his sin, and a desire to flee from the wrath to come. But in the case of those whom I am addressing, I mean those who are anxious about salvation, this is already done; they are convinced of sin, and desirous to flee from impending judgment. What more is necessary to prepare them to believe in Christ? But what is meant by those who talk thus, is, that there must be a long course of conviction; a production and growth of early affections; a series of holy actions; an expansion of religious knowledge; and that then, and not until then, sinners are encouraged to trust in Christ, and hope for salvation. Now, it is very true, that every sinner, in coming to Christ by faith, must be prepared and ready to give up every sin. He must be willing to sacrifice sins that may be as pleasant as a right eye, and as useful as a right hand. He must be willing to take up his cross, and follow Christ to bonds, imprisonment, and death. He must consider himself as "called unto holiness"—and this is his state of mind, as soon as he is really convinced of sin. What more in the way of preparation for pardon does he need? Is not a man prepared for forgiveness, as soon as he is convinced of his transgression?

If a father promises pardon to an offending child as soon as he shall confess his fault, has that child any need to say, "I will prepare myself for pardon by a long course of future good conduct?" His father is ready to forgive him, and he of course is ready to be forgiven, upon the very first moment of true penitence. If God had said he would not pardon us, until months or years of good conduct had taken place, he would have been only mocking us; for what good conduct can we perform until he has received us into his favor, and bestowed upon us his Spirit? The first concern of a sinner is, or should be, to be pardoned; the second, to be holy; and he should desire the first, in order to the second. *It is a radical error to suppose that sanctification goes before justification.* We must first be justified, before we can be sanctified. Mark this well. I repeat it, that you may notice and weigh it well, *we must be justified before we can be sanctified.* We are justified by faith; and without faith we cannot please God; consequently, until we believe, we can perform no good works; and when we believe, we are accepted of God. Faith, then, is *immediately* our duty, without waiting for any preparatory process. But, perhaps, this will be made still more plain by a reference to examples.

Take then the conversions, or at least some of them, recorded in Scripture. Take the case of the penitent thief[4]. What preparatory process went on in this man's mind heart and conduct, beyond the work of the Spirit, in convincing him of sin? He appears to have thought of his sin, and repented for the first time, when he was crucified; and at almost the same moment believed in Christ, and entertained a hope of mercy.

---

4   Luke 23:40-43

Read the account of the three thousand converted on the day of Pentecost (Acts 2). Up to the time when they heard Peter's sermon, they were the murderers of Christ; by that sermon they were convinced of sin, and that same day they were rejoicing in the assurance of pardon. Now what preparatory process was carried on in their hearts, beyond the work of the Spirit in convincing them of sin?

Consider the conversion of the apostle Paul, who was a bloody persecutor; and a day or two after, not only a pardoned sinner, a baptized believer, a rejoicing Christian, but a consecrated apostle. What preparatory process in the way of long-cherished convictions, or holy actions, was there in him? (Acts 8)

Consult the narrative of the Philippian jailor (Acts 16:25-34). In the same night he was convinced of sin, he believed in Christ, he was filled with peace, and was baptized. When, in agony of soul, he cried out, "What must I do to be saved?" his heaven-inspired teacher replied, "Believe on the Lord Jesus Christ, and you shall be saved." The apostle did not speak to him of any preparatory process, any long course of prescribed duties, any training for his reception by Christ, but simply said, "Believe;" and he meant, of course, believe now! And so the trembling penitent understood him, for he believed at once, and entered into peace.

I bring forward these instances, (and almost all the other cases of conversion spoken of in the New Testament are of a similar nature,) to prove, not that all conversions are equally sudden and remarkable, but only this one point—that no other preparation in the sinner's mind is necessary, in order to his believing and being justified, but a real conviction of sin. As soon as a man knows he is a lost sinner, that is, is truly convinced of his state of condemnation, he is required to believe in Christ, and to hope for pardon—then he is in a state, a *fit* state, to receive it; and moreover, he would not be, and could not be, more fit by waiting ten years in the most agonizing convictions, or the most holy performance of duty. The sinner is condemned, and is any moment after conviction in a state to be reprieved; and he can never begin to perform the acts of a good citizen until he is justified. Faith is the very first act of evangelical obedience which anyone can render to God—and it is the spring of all others. We never can be holy until we believe in Christ; and, therefore, all ideas of preparation for coming to Christ are erroneous, arise from mistaken views of the way of a sinner's acceptance with God, and are generally to be traced to a principle of self-righteousness.

This, perhaps, will be the case with many who will read these pages; they will want to be more prepared, either by convictions or by holiness, for coming to Christ; that is, they will want something of their own in which to glory; something to give them courage and confidence in approaching the Savior; something to render them less dependent on free, sovereign grace; something to entitle them, if not to salvation, at least to the righteousness of Christ as the meritorious cause of it. Anxious inquirer! you know not the secret workings of pride and self-righteousness in your soul; you are not yet acquainted with the deceitfulness of the human heart; you are ignorant of the artifices of Satan, or you would detect in those longings after some preparatory process a scheme of the enemy of souls to keep you from Christ; yes, it is a veil to hide from your view the glory of his cross, and a stumbling-block to hinder you from approaching the fountain of life. Wait no longer "If you tarry until you're better, you will never come at all."

It is of infinite consequence for you to remember, that you are received, not as worthy, but as unworthy; not as favorites, but as those who have been enemies; not as deserving life by your convictions, but as sentenced to death for your transgressions. "To him that works not, but believes on him who justifies *the ungodly*, his faith is counted for righteousness" (Rom 4:5). Mark that expression; there is a vast comprehension of subject in it; it is the key to a correct knowledge of justification; "believes in him who justifies the *ungodly*." We are justified, so far as we are concerned, under the character of "ungodly." If, then, we seek to make ourselves godly before we come to Christ, and wish to come under that character—we are shutting ourselves out from the blessing of justification; for this is granted only to them who consider themselves ungodly.

3. Another mistake into which inquirers fall in the commencement of a religious course is, *to indulge a misplaced solicitude about the evidences of personal religion.* I know that the sacred writers speak much and often on the subject of evidences of personal religion. But a person must *have* true religion before he can possess the evidence of it; and at present your solicitude should be rather to *be* Christians—than to know you are such. It is, however, a very common case for people, as soon as they begin to be concerned about religion, to begin also to be anxious to find out the marks of salvation in themselves. Hence they are ever microscopically analyzing all their feelings, watching their motives, reviewing their conduct; sometimes hoping, when they see, or think they see, a good mark; but more generally desponding, as the result of seeing so much that is positively wrong, or really defective in the state of their hearts. I wish you to attend to this remark—"*That inquirers after salvation should be much more occupied in looking to Christ, than in looking into their own hearts*—and that when they do look into themselves, it should be for conviction, and not for consolation."

Consider the case of the Israelites, when bitten by the fiery serpents in the wilderness. Moses, you know, was ordered to make a brazen serpent, and elevate it upon a pole, and whoever looked upon the brazen serpent lived. "Look and live," was the mandate and promise. Now cannot you fancy you see the poor poisoned creatures, straining their very eyes in gazing upon the object appointed for their healing? Do you think they spent all their time, or much of their time, or any of it—in examining the wounds, to see if they were healing? Were they so foolish as to look off from the means of cure, to ascertain their progress in recovery? No, they would not have taken their eye from the brazen serpent to look at a second sun, if it had been at that time kindled in the firmament. Their eye was fixed; and as they looked, they felt their pain assuaged; their fever cooled; their health returning. If they looked away from the brazen serpent, they felt in danger of relapse; and in this way they recovered.

Thus should it be with the sinner; he should look to Jesus —healing is *there*; and is obtained, not by looking to see if it is come, or is coming. The more the mind is fixed on Christ, the more clear its views are of his mediatorial work, the more steady and fixed the eye of faith is on the cross of him who was lifted up, "that whoever believes in him should not perish, but have eternal life," the firmer will be the consciousness of the soul that it *does* believe, and the more abundant will be all the fruits and evidences of faith. The Israelite had no doubt of his healing as long as he looked to the brazen serpent, for he felt it going on; nor will the soul doubt of its acceptance with God, so long as it looks to Christ. "He who believes on the Son of God has the witness in himself," not only of the truth of Christianity, but of his own personal religion. The way to have our evidences increased, is to have our faith increased; and the way to have our faith increased, is not by looking *into ourselves,* who are the subjects of faith—but *out of ourselves* to Christ, who is the object of faith.

Faith is the mainspring and regulator of all the graces; our joy, our love, our hope, will all be in proportion to our faith. And our faith can never be strengthened by an anxious and constant poring over the feelings of our hearts. Nor can our faith be strengthened merely by determining to be strong in faith; but by an intelligent and increasingly clear view of the person and work of Christ. "How long," said David, "shall I take counsel in my soul, having sorrow in my heart daily?" He tells us almost immediately after how he got rid of his grief, even by looking away from himself—to God. "I have trusted in your mercy, my heart shall rejoice in your salvation" (Psa.13:2-5). The first evidence of faith is the peace of mind that it brings to the soul, or the relief which it affords from the burden of sin. The next evidence of faith is holiness; but there can be neither peace nor holiness until there is faith. Many people, I apprehend, are greatly deceived in their supposed object in seeking for marks of conversion; it is not *evidence* of faith they are seeking after, but *matter* of faith; not evidence that they have received the righteousness of Christ, but evidence out of which they may make a righteousness of their own. They want comfort, and instead of looking for it in Christ —they are looking for it in themselves. Hence, when they have found, or think they have found, a good mark in themselves, they rejoice in it, as those that have found great spoil.

Doubting, dejected, and anxious sinner, you have been reading, thinking, hearing, praying, striving, examining, consulting books upon evidences, and lists of marks of salvation, inquiring of others how they feel, and what they conclude to be evidence of a work of grace. And yet you are as far from any satisfactory conclusion, as to your state, as ever; like the beast in the mire, all your striving seems but to sink you deeper and deeper. Now then take another plan, since your own has failed, and instead of troubling yourself about evidences—look to Christ! Keep your eye fixed on him; meditate upon the Divinity of his person; the sufficiency of his atonement; the perfection of his righteousness; the riches of his grace; the universality of his invitations. Look at the *object* of faith, the *grounds* of faith, the *warrant* of faith; the more you do this, the stronger your faith will become; and the stronger your faith is, the greater your peace will be.

Instead of laboring to love Christ, and becoming dejected that you do not love him more, take another course, and dwell upon the love of Christ to you. Meditate on his amazing grace, his most wonderful compassion, not only to the world in general, but to you, as part of the world; labor and pray to be "able to comprehend with all saints, what is the breadth, and length, and depth, and height, and to know the love of Christ, which passes knowledge." This, this is the way to grow in love to him; for if we love him, it is because he first loved us. It is a great principle which I am concerned to impress upon you, that subjective religion, or, in other words, religion in us, is produced and sustained by fixing the mind on objective religion, or the facts and doctrines of the word of God. Neither evidences nor comfort should be sought directly, or on their own account, or as separate things, but as the result of faith. Take this as an important sentiment, that the subject of evidences belongs more to the believer than to the inquirer; to the Christian, who professes to be already in the way, and not to the concerned seeker after the way.

4. But there is another mistake which inquirers are apt to make, which, though nearly allied to what I have already stated, is sufficiently distinct to justify a separate consideration of it, and that is, *confounding faith and assurance.* Faith is such a cordial belief that Christ died for sinners, as leads me to a dependence upon him for my salvation. Assurance, as the word is usually understood in religious discourse, means a persuasion that I *do* so believe, and am in a state of salvation. Faith means a belief that Christ is willing to receive me. Assurance means conviction that he *has received* me; that, in short, I am a Christian. Now it is manifest that these two are different from each other. One of them, that is, faith, signifying the performance of

an action, or coming into a certain state. And assurance, signifies the consciousness that *I have* come into that state.

It is also equally evident that faith must precede assurance. We must first believe that Christ died for sinners, before we can know that we have believed. The first simple act of faith is a belief that Christ died for all sinners, for the whole world; the next, as arising out of it, if it be not indeed included in it, is that he died for us as part of the world. "I believe," says the sinner, who is coming with confidence to Christ, "that God so loved the world, that he gave his only begotten Son, that whoever believes in him should not perish, but have everlasting life. Then, as I am a part of the world, I believe he loved me, and is willing to save me." This is faith. The soul then feels joy and peace in believing, love to God, gratitude to Christ, hatred of sin, subjugation of the world, fellowship with the righteous. "Now," says the man, "*I know* I believe, I am conscious both of the act of believing, and also of its gracious effects." This is assurance.

I may illustrate the subject by referring again to the rebellious subjects and their gracious sovereign. The ringleader of a revolt can scarcely persuade himself that he can be included in the act of amnesty; he reads the proclamation again, which runs thus—'The king, pitying his deluded subjects, and filled with clemency, will grant a gracious pardon to whoever will lay down their arms by such a day.' Having examined the proofs of the authenticity of the act, and being satisfied on that point, he says, "It is really true, and I believe that the king is willing to pardon *all* that submit; and as he has made no exception against any, but says—*Whoever* will lay down his arms shall be forgiven, I believe that there is mercy for me." Thus far faith goes; and even before he reaches the scene of pardon, or takes a step towards it, his mind is at rest. The proclamation itself, as soon as it is understood and believed, gives him comfort; he has no doubt of his being accepted. He goes and lays

down his arms, and now he is assured he is safe; he is conscious he has done what the monarch required, and he feels he
has what the monarch promised.

In his case, however, you perceive that there would not be
much solicitude about assurance. Faith, and compliance with
the monarch's demand, would be all that he would concern
himself about. Assurance would follow upon faith and action.
So should it be with anxious inquirers after salvation—their
business is to believe, what? that they are Christians? No! For
a belief that I am a Christian is not faith, but assurance. But we
are to believe the Gospel, which is God's proclamation of mercy and pardon to his rebel subjects—they are to feel persuaded
that God has *loved* them in common with other sinners, invited
them, and promised to receive *them*, and take the comfort of
this revelation of mercy; and then, from the pacifying effect of
this upon their conscience, and the purifying effect of it upon
their hearts—to be assured they have believed, and have
passed from death unto life. Faith then is not assurance, but the
cause of it.

Now, inquirer, are you not aware that you have confound-
ed these two; and have been consequently walking in great
perplexity? You are dejected, and cannot be comforted. Why?
"Oh," you say, "my faith is so weak; indeed, I am afraid I have
no faith." Now, what do you mean by having no faith? "I am
afraid I am not a Christian. I fear I do not believe. I am full of
unbelief." But let me tell you, that you never can be delivered
from distress in this way. You are wanting to know you are a
Christian before you *are* one. You are striving to know you are
a believer before you believe. You wish to be assured you are
accepted of Christ, in order that you may go to him for acceptance. Faith is not believing that you are a Christian, but believing that Christ died for sinners. Unbelief is not doubting
that you are a Christian, but doubting Christ's willingness to
save you. My advice to you then is, to leave assurance, as a

first matter, out of consideration; to talk nothing, and think nothing, about it. Your business, at present, is with faith—you are to believe; you are to trust your soul upon the atonement of Christ; you are to be persuaded that he died for sinners, died for *you*, and is willing to save *you*. This is the assurance you are to seek; and this is what the apostle means by the full assurance of faith; an unhesitating confidence that the Lord Jesus is able and willing to save to the uttermost; and, therefore, able and willing to save you. Get your mind full of conviction of the truth of this; let your soul be thrown, as it were, wide open, to admit this delightful persuasion, that Christ is mighty to save; delighted to save; waiting to save all, you among the rest; you as willingly as any of the rest; and then this truth will give you such peace, and exert such a power over your heart, as to prove to you the existence and reality of your faith. The assurance which the Scriptures speak of is the assurance of God's love to you in Christ; and this, I again say, is the only assurance which you have to do with at present.

CHAPTER SEVEN

Perplexities

Often Felt By Inquirers

1. MANY are exceedingly perplexed and distressed *on the subject of their personal 'election' to eternal life.* I have nothing to do now with those careless or profane people, who make this solemn doctrine, or rather profess to make it, an excuse, for the entire neglect of religion; and who, with wicked indifference, exclaim, "If I am elected to be saved, I *shall* be saved, without any concern of mine; but if I am *not* elected, no effort of mine will or can save me." The fact is, that such people do not believe in the doctrine of election at all; nor, indeed, care anything about salvation, but are utterly ignorant and careless, and refer to this solemn truth, either to quiet their own conscience, or to silence and turn away the voice of faithful admonition. But there are others who do feel, especially in the early stages of religious inquiry, no small degree of perplexity on this subject. Now, here let me at once inform you, that *you*, who are inquiring after salvation, have nothing to do with the doctrine of election. Nor, indeed, has anyone anything to do with the secret purposes of God, as a *rule of conduct.*

The sublime truth of God's sovereignty in the salvation of his people is introduced in Scripture, not to discourage the approach of the sinner to Christ for salvation, but to remind those who *have* come to him, that their salvation is all of grace; to take away from them all ground of boasting; to confirm their faith in the accomplishment of the Divine promises; to promote their comfort; to inculcate the necessity of personal holiness; and to encourage Christians amidst the afflictions of life, Rom. 8:9; Ephes. 1:4, 5, 9, 11; 1 Peter 1:2.

But it was never designed to be a source of discouragement to penitents. The rule of your conduct is the invitation and promise of Christ—not the secret purposes of God—"The secret things belong unto the Lord our God; but those things which are revealed belong unto us and to our children forever, that we may do all the words of this law." The mercy of God is infinite; the merit of Christ's atonement is infinite; the power of the Spirit is infinite; and the invitations of the Gospel are universal. "Come unto me, *all* who labor and are heavy laden." And thus says the Lord, "I have no pleasure in the death of the wicked." "The Lord is longsuffering to us—not willing that any should perish, but that all should come to repentance." "Him that comes to me, I will in never cast out." "Whoever will, let him take the water of life freely." Now, these are the words of Scripture, and must, therefore, be true—and *here* is the rule of your conduct.

You can understand this, but you know nothing about the secret purposes of God. Besides, if you knew you were elected, you would not be received and saved because of this knowledge, but because you believed in Christ, who invites men, not as elected to life, but as lost sinners condemned to death. If you had been permitted to read the decrees of heaven, and had seen your name in the Lamb's book of life, you would not be one whit more welcome to Christ than you are now that you know nothing about the matter. You are *invited*; and if you neglect the invitation which you do know, because of a decree which you do not know—the blame of perishing will lie at your own door; and you will find at last that you are lost, not in consequence of any purpose of God determining you to be lost, but in consequence of your own unbelief.

Why should the purpose of God, in reference to salvation, be that only view of the Divine decree that perplexes you? Do you not believe there is also a purpose which refers to the events of your natural life and death? But do you, on this account, hesitate in sickness to take the medicine prescribed for you by a skillful physician, lest you should not be ordained to life? No! You say, and with reason, "I know nothing about the Divine purpose; my business is with plain rules of duty, and with instituted means; for if I am to live, I can expect recovery only by these means." Act thus in reference to your souls; leave God's decrees out of consideration, for you know nothing about them, and have nothing to do with them.

You are invited to use the means of life; if you are decreed to be saved, you must be saved by them; and if you use them aright, you certainly *will* be saved. If any use at all is to be made, by an inquirer, of the doctrine of election, it is a use in his own favor. You know not that you are *not* elected, and the very solicitude of your mind about salvation is a presumption that you *are*, since that solicitude is the way in which God carries his decree into execution. Besides, if you get away from the invitation, and instead of making that the rule of your conduct, trouble your head with other views and subjects, you will find as much perplexity in God's *foreknowledge* as you do in his decrees. Even those who deny the purposes of God have just as much reason to perplex themselves with Divine foreknowledge, and say, "Whatever God foresees, and nothing but what he foresees, will take place; now he foresees either that I *shall* be saved or lost; and as I do not know that he foresees that I shall be saved, I am greatly discouraged." Abandon at once, therefore, all solicitude, and indeed all thoughts about the decree, and fix you attention on the *invitation.* Christ bids you come to him for salvation; and every bar and obstacle which lies in the way of your coming is placed there by you—

and not by him. He does not say, Come when you have ascertained your election; but, Come and ascertain it. He does not say, You are welcome if you have read the decree; but, You are welcome if you believe the promise. He does not say, Come under the presumption that you are predestinated; but, Come with the assurance that you are bidden. Your business is to make your calling sure, and then you will no longer doubt of your *election*.

2. Another source of perplexity with some is, a fear that they have committed the unpardonable blasphemy against the Holy Spirit. This is by no means an uncommon ground of painful solicitude; and even when it does not amount to a deep and terrifying conviction, yet the subject haunts the imagination with many distressing fears, keeps the mind unsettled, and prevents that calm and tranquilizing reliance to which the penitent is invited. Now, I wish you to know that in whatever solemn and terrific obscurity this subject is enveloped, no one that is really concerned about his salvation need to be under the least fear that he has passed the line of hope, and entered the region where mercy never dispenses pardon; the very fear of having committed this sin, when such fear is connected with concern about true religion, is a proof that it has *not* been committed. It may be taken for granted, that in every case where this mysterious crime has been committed, the transgressor is given up either to a deadly stupor or a raging frenzy of the conscience.

But perhaps, the best way of removing the apprehension is to explain the subject which occasions it. What is the nature of this sin? Read the account of it—"Therefore I say unto you, All manner of sin and blasphemy shall be forgiven unto men; but the *blasphemy* against the Holy Spirit shall not be forgiven unto men. And whoever speaks a word against the Son of man, it shall be forgiven him; but whoever *speaks* against the Holy Spirit, it shall not be forgiven him, neither in this world, neither in the world to come" (Matt.12:31,32). The occasion of

these solemn words was the conduct of the Pharisees, in ascribing the miracles of Christ, the reality of which they could
not deny or doubt, to the power of the devil. Still, though this
was the occasion of the words, it was not a description of the
sin; for this was speaking against *the Son of man*, and not
against the Holy Spirit, which was not yet poured out. (It is
proper to remark here, that very many wise and good men are
of opinion, that this awful crime referred as truly to the miracles wrought by Christ during his personal ministry, as to those
which were wrought by the Holy Spirit, through the instrumen-
tality of the apostles, on and after the day of Pentecost.)

The day of Pentecost, properly speaking, commenced the
dispensation of the Spirit; when his Divine gifts, conferred
upon the apostles, completed the evidence of the Christian
economy; and the language of Christ, therefore, seemed to direct the Pharisees forward, in the way of impressive warning,
to that event; and to remind them, though they understood him
not, that the malicious contempt cast upon *his* miracles, if repeated after the *Holy Spirit* was poured out, would fill the measure of their iniquities, seal them up in unbelief, and place
them beyond the reach of mercy. There would remain no further evidence of the Divine mission of Christ; the last and the
fullest attestation to his Messiahship would be rejected and re-
viled with malice of heart.

If, in addition to this, you will just recollect the meaning
of the term blasphemy, which signifies to speak reproachfully,
opprobriously, or impiously, you will then have the nature of
this crime before you. It is knowledge in the mind that miracles were wrought; malice in the heart against Christ, in attestation of whom they were given; contempt of the Holy Spirit,
their author; and the language of spite upon the tongue, revil-
ing the miracles themselves, by ascribing them to the agency
of devils. It is not simple unbelief under the dispensation of the
Spirit, persevered in until death; it is not mere infidelity, even
under very aggravated circumstances; but it is the union of

conviction, malice, and impiety. It is therefore evident, that *if* this sin is *now ever* committed, no inquirer after salvation needs for a moment entertain any apprehension that it has been committed by *him*. *He* has not passed the boundary of mercy; nor is there any sin he has ever been guilty of, however enormous in magnitude, or however painful in remembrance, but the blood of Jesus Christ can cleanse it away.

3. *But this leads me to another perplexity, which is felt by others; who, though they do not fear that they have been guilty of this unpardonable crime, are distressed by the apprehension that their sins are too great, too numerous, or too atrocious to be forgiven.*

Sometimes convinced sinners are enabled by Divine grace to indulge the hope of pardon, almost as soon as they receive the conviction of sin. Yes, some are led to see the evil of sin at first, more by the mercy of the gospel, than the stern justice which appears in the law; but others are long and sorely harassed by fears of rejection, before they are brought to a comfortable expectation of forgiveness. This is more commonly the case with those who have gone to great lengths in sin, and have resisted the clearest and loudest warnings of conscience; it is not unusual for such people, when truly awakened to a sense of their sin and danger, to plunge into the very depths of despondency, and to remain for a long time without hope or peace.

In some cases, I think it possible that this desponding frame of mind is really *cherished*, as if it were an evidence of sincere and deep repentance—there are those who look upon doubts and fears as the marks of a work of grace, and proofs of genuine piety. This, however, is a great delusion, since true godly sorrow is both accompanied and promoted by faith and hope. Despair tends to harden the heart, and to freeze up the feelings of penitence. God cannot be glorified, nor Christ honored, by doubting of his ability or willingness to save. I am persuaded that many people say more about their sins being too great to be pardoned, than they either believe or feel, from a supposition that it is a token of humility to talk thus. Watch against this, for it is an act of guilty insincerity—it is trifling with sacred things, and should be avoided.

But there are many who are *really* distressed with the most painful solicitude, and the most gloomy apprehensions, about the pardon of their sins. Now here let me put a plain question to you—Is your concern merely to be *pardoned*, or to be sanctified as well as pardoned? Are you afraid only of being left under the punishment of sin, or do you also fear being left under its power? If you are so selfish as to be concerned for nothing but your own safety, without caring for holiness, no wonder you are left by God to such dark despondency. You do not yet understand the design of Christ's work, which is not merely to deliver from hell, but also from sin. Change, then, or rather *enlarge* the object of your hope, so as to include sanctification as well as justification, and in all probability your unbelief and distress will soon give way; for it will be found easier, perhaps, to some to believe that God is willing to make them holy, than to forgive them. Desponding sinner, think of this; the salvation of Christ is designed to make you a new creature, and to restore the image of God to your soul; and do you not believe that God must be infinitely willing to do *this*?

After all, however, there are some, who, even with this view of the design of Christ's death, cannot be induced to hope that their sins can be forgiven—none have sinned, they think, like them; there are aggravations in their sins, not to be found in the conduct of any other. Now I refer such burdened and desponding minds, *to the promises of God's word.* Read attentively such declarations as are found in the following passages —Isaiah 44:22; Isaiah 55:6, 7; Micah 7:18, 19; Matthew 12:31, 32. Dwell, especially, upon this last passage, because it most explicitly declares that the blasphemy against the Holy Spirit is the only sin excepted from forgiveness. If, then, you are led to see that you have not committed the only sin for which there is no forgiveness, it must, I think, appear plain to you, that your transgressions are not unpardonable.

Dwell much upon the perfection of Christ's work in making atonement for sin. The apostle declares that "the blood of Jesus Christ *cleanses* from all sin" (1 John 1:7). It would seem as if this declaration were written on purpose to meet such cases as yours. This scripture says positively, the blood of christ *cleanses* from *all sin.* "No," you say, in flat and perverse contradiction, "it cannot cleanse from mine." Did Christ die to save sinners, and yet are there some sinners to be found, according to your view, whom he *cannot* save? Then his work of salvation is unfinished, and his character as a Savior is incomplete. Has he not already saved millions by the merit of his death? Well, suppose all the sins of those millions had been in you alone, could he not as easily have saved you, in that case, as he has saved them? Certainly he could. Can you really make up your mind to go and say to Christ, "Lord, you *cannot,* will *not,* save *me*; there is neither love enough in your heart, nor power enough in your Spirit, nor merit enough in your great sacrifice, to save me. Look upon *me,* and behold a sinner whom even *you* cannot save—behold in me a sinner whom your utmost ability cannot reach."

No! You cannot say this; and yet you might say it, and innocently say it, if what you affirm were true, that your sins are too great to be forgiven. Let it be admitted, for the sake of argument, that you are the chief of sinners, still Christ can save you; so at least the apostle thought, when he said, *"The saying is faithful and worthy of all acceptance, that Christ Jesus came into the world to save sinners; of whom I am chief." And read what follows:* "However, for this cause I obtained mercy, that in me first (or as it signifies, in me the chief sinner), Jesus Christ might display all his patience, for an example of those who were going to believe in him for eternal life" (1 Timothy 1:15-16).

Think what Saul of Tarsus was; a bloody persecutor, and even murderer of the disciples of Christ; yet Christ not only pardoned him, but raised him to the dignity of the chief of the apostles. For what purpose? To be a pattern of God's mercy to the end of time. Yes, there he stands, upon the pedestal of his own immortal writings, a monument of the riches, power, and sovereignty of Divine grace, bearing this inscription *"I, who was a blasphemer, a persecutor, and injurious, obtained mercy. Let no man ever despair; for if there arises a greater sinner than I was, let him look on me, and hope for pardon through the blood of Christ. I was forgiven, to encourage the wickedest of men to repent, to believe in Jesus, and expect salvation."*

Consider well the other instances recorded in the word of God, of pardon granted to some of the greatest sinners. There is scarcely one class of sinners, or one kind of crime, which is not specifically mentioned in Scripture as having been pardoned. Think of Manasseh, an apostate, an idolater, a wholesale murderer, a man whose example and authority as a king were employed to fill his nation with iniquity. Think of David, who was guilty of the united crimes of adultery and murder. Think of of the dying malefactor, who was saved upon his cross. Think of of the Jews who were converted on the day of Pentecost, and who, though they had been the murderers of Christ, were forgiven. Think of of the once polluted members of the Corinthian church, 1 Cor. 6:9, 11. What proofs are these that no sins will keep a man from salvation, that do not keep him from Christ.

The fact is, that our sins being great or little, few or many, has nothing to do with this matter, in the way of making it more difficult or more easy to obtain mercy. No man is pardoned because his sins are fewer; and none is rejected because his sins are more. Great sinners are as welcome as little ones; for as the skill of the physician is the more displayed in dangerous and difficult cases, than in slight ones, so is the grace of Christ the more illustriously manifested in the pardon and sanctification of notorious sinners, than in the salvation of those who have not gone so far astray. If God's mercy is infinite, it must be as easy to him to pardon a million of sins as one. Desponding sinner, dry up your tears, and doubt no longer. The greatest sin you can commit is to disbelieve God's promise to forgive your other sins. Unbelief is the most *heinous* of all sins. *"He who believes not God, <u>has made him a liar"</u>* (1 John 5:10). Yes, you are giving God the lie to his face, as often as you say your sins are too great to be forgiven. Do you not tremble at this? Is there not abominable pride in unbelief? Who and what are you, that you should suppose God has any object or interest in deceiving *you* by a false promise? Are you so considerable a person, that God should think it worth his while to falsify his word, in order to draw you into false confidence? Believe, then, from this hour, that God is more willing to forgive you the greatest of your sins, than you imagine he is to blot out the least of them.

4. *Some are perplexed with the notion, that as "the sacrifice of the wicked is an abomination to God," and as none of the works of unregenerate people are acceptable to God, that it is not right for them to pray, since they are not yet believers in Christ.* With regard to the expression above alluded to, which speaks of the sacrifice of the wicked, it means the hypocritical religious services of men who are still living in the commission of known sin, and impiously designing to make some atonement for their iniquities by their sacrifices. This is evident from the passage itself, where it is also said, "The way of the wicked is abomination," that is, his conduct; and because his conduct is abominable, therefore his prayer is also abominable. This passage is best expounded by a reference to Isaiah 1:10, 18. It applies to a totally different case from yours.

I acknowledge that your prayers do not merit the Divine blessing which you are concerned to obtain, however frequently or fervently they may be presented. You ought not to pray with the idea that there is any worth in your prayers to make any atonement for your sins; nor ought you to look for peace and comfort from your prayers. I go a step further, and remind you that, unless you pray in faith, your prayers are not such as God has engaged to answer. You should believe that God is willing and waiting to bestow all spiritual blessing, for he has promised to do so. To doubt at the time you pray whether God will grant what he has promised, is sin; but to doubt whether it is your duty to pray, because you do not yet know that you are accepted of God, is unquestionably wrong. You may as well question whether it is your duty to read the Bible—or to go to public worship. Did not Peter tell Simon Magus to pray? "Repent, therefore," said he, "of this your wickedness, and pray God if perhaps the thought of your heart may be forgiven you; for I perceive that you are in the gall of bitterness, and in the bond of iniquity" (Acts 8:22-23). And we read of many instances in the Old Testament of people praying, and being heard and answered, who were not at the time truly converted to God; as, for example, Ahab, 1 Kings 21:29; Jehoahaz, 2 Kings 13:4, 5. So also the Ninevites prayed, and obtained favor of God, Jonah 3:5, 10. No prayers can be acceptable to God that are insincere; and such are the prayers of wicked men for salvation, for they do not really desire to be saved from sin. But the prayers of the inquirer after salvation are sincere; he really desires it.

Still, however, I would remind you, that as long as you pray in an unconverted state, your prayers are only the operations of self-love, which, though not sinful, are not truly holy; they are but the cries of misery after relief, the desire of the soul after happiness; and, however frequently or fervently repeated, prefer no *claim* on God for his blessing. The sin lies not in praying; for, if sincere, there is no sin in crying to God for help; but in not believing. Instead, therefore, of leaving off prayer, or harassing your minds with doubts about the propriety of carrying it on, continue instant in prayer, believing at the same time the promise of mercy in Christ Jesus. You are to add to your prayer, faith; and it is doubtless your duty at once to believe—but if your soul loses not immediately its guilty fears, still you are to go on praying for mercy, and for faith to receive it.

It cannot be wrong for a soul to cry for mercy. With such light as you have, although it may not be such as is necessary to salvation, lift up your desire to God. Pray for more knowledge, stronger faith, and firmer hope. Prayer is your duty, and it is your privilege; and let no speculative difficulties have a moment's influence to induce you to suspend it. If you cannot yet pray as a believer, cry for mercy as a sinner. But do not remain in unbelief, supposing that prayer can be a substitute for faith; for, as I said before, so I repeat, God does not bind himself to answer any prayers but those of faith.

CHAPTER EIGHT

Discouragements
Which Present Themselves at the Commencement of a Pious Course

THE word of God teaches us to expect these. What means "the strait gate," but an entrance attended with difficulty? What means "counting the cost," but contemplating obstacles, and preparing to meet them? Bunyan knew the course to heaven, when he placed the slough of despond in the first stage of the journey. You are mistaken if you expect by one easy stride to reach the firm and solid ground beyond this dismal swamp. Sincerity will diminish difficulties and finally overcome them, but it will not prevent them. Prepare then, for discouragement, for you will be sure to meet with it; and it is both wise and merciful to forewarn you of it, lest you should conclude that some strange thing has happened to you. But observe, *no part of this discouragement comes from God.* He interposes no obstacle, raises no difficulty, presents no objection. A doubt of *His* willingness to save, a suspicion of his mercy, would be fatal to your hopes. But all is clear ground, so far as God is concerned. Dwell on this thought, it is a blissful one; ponder it, before you go another step; arm yourselves to meet every discouragement, come from what quarter it may, with this conviction, that God waits to be gracious; yes, like the father in the parable of the prodigal son, he is out, looking for you; his infinite mercy is in motion towards you; he comes to you faster than you go to him. What then is your discouragement?

1. *The cold indifference, the repulsive shyness, of professing Christians.* You thought that the very look of concern, the very countenance that seemed to say to their eyes, if not to their ears, "What shall I do to be saved?" would draw the sympathies of many upon you; instead of which, you are left without a friend to commiserate, guide, or soothe you, and are compelled, in the agony of your soul, to say, even to the multitude that go up to Zion, "Is it nothing to you, all you that pass by? Come, see, if there be any sorrow like unto mine. Will no man care for my soul?" Ah, my friend, let me tell you in the beginning of your career, *that you cannot expect too little from man, nor too much from God.* It is the scandal of the Church of Christ, and in some measure also of its ministers, *that serious inquirers after salvation are shamefully neglected.* But shall this discourage you? What, when all heaven is interested on your behalf? When Father, Son, and Holy Spirit are concerned for you? When the blessed angels are rejoicing over you, and flying on wings of love to minister to you, as an heir of salvation? Cast away your gloom, look to God; and if the neglect of Christians should lead you to a more simple dependence upon Christ, you will be a gainer in the end. Too many friends, and too much attention, might do you injury, by leading you to depend too much upon an arm of flesh.

2. *Many are discouraged by witnessing the low state of piety among professors.* They see no counterpart to their own concern among those who have long borne the Christian name. While they themselves are crying, "What shall we do to be saved?" they hear little from the lips of many Christian professors, but, "What shall we eat and drink? How shall we be adorn ourselves? What is the news of the day?" They see so much worldly-mindedness, so much imperfection of temper, so

many things unworthy of the Christian character, that they can scarcely believe there is reality in religion, and are sometimes ready to give it all up as a mere name. Nay, from some of these very professors they receive plain hints that they are too concerned, too precise, too earnest and urgent. Oh, you wicked professors! you child-murderers! (for by what softer name can I call you, in thus attempting to strangle the children of God in their birth?) I beseech you to consider the mischief you are doing, and abandon this effort to extinguish the solicitude of souls beginning to feel the energies of spiritual life.

And, you inquirers after salvation, do not be discouraged. If these men are living below their profession, that is their business, not yours. Salvation is necessary for *you*, whether they are sincere and earnest in seeking it or not. It will be no compensation for the loss of your soul, to think that they lost theirs. If there were not yet one real Christian in all the world, this would be no excuse for your neglecting to become one. Look into the Bible, rather than to professors. Instead of giving up the matter, you should gather this inference from what you see, that it is no easy thing to be a Christian. Should the bad tempers, the unworthy conduct of professors induce you to relinquish the pursuit of salvation, it will be poor consolation in the bottomless pit to look back upon the cause of your ruin.

3. *You are, perhaps, discouraged by the prospect of opposition from your nearest friends.* You see them all worldly, and plainly perceive that your real conversion to God will place you in direct opposition to them—that your becoming a Christian, and acting as such, will bring into your house the scene described by our Lord, Matt. 10:34-38. "Oh," say you, "how fearful is the prospect before me! my piety will sound a note of discord in a family where all has been peace until now, although a peace founded on a common disregard of religion; and will introduce confusion and strife where all has been union and harmony." "I must brave the anger of my husband,"

says the wife, "and perhaps alienate that heart, on which my spirit has hitherto reposed with such delight." Or, says the child, "I must seem to be disobedient to a parent, whom I have hitherto found it to be my duty and bliss to obey. Oh, *can* I do it? Is there no other way to heaven? Are there no milder terms of submission to the authority of Christ?" None! None whatever!

I do not conceal that Christianity is a difficult path. I should be destitute of all sympathy, my friend, if I did not feel for you. But I dare not withdraw the cross. My soul would perish with yours, if I successfully attempted to persuade you that, in your circumstances, repentance, faith, the love of God, and all the other graces and virtues included in decided spiritual religion, could be dispensed with. God *will* not, cannot, relax his demands, and I dare not. Husband and wife, parent and child, houses and lands, worldly reputation, and the applause of men, must all give place to Him. He demands the heart; and he has infinite compensation to make for all you sacrifice for him. He will make the crown infinitely more valuable than the cross is terrible. You may be, you ought to be, discreet in your profession; you must avoid all unnecessary opposition to the wishes of unconverted relatives. You should, if possible, be ten times more obliging, more devoted, more sweetly kind, in all other matters. You should return good for evil. You should exhibit the most undisturbed meekness. You should try to conquer their violence by patience—but y*ou must not, you dare not,* give up your convictions. You must be willing to die of a broken heart, and by the wrongs of persecution, rather than give up your pursuit of salvation. Trust in God, he will support you. If he calls you to be a martyr in this way, he will first give you a martyr's faith, and then a martyr's crown. Let the following impressive fact be read by you with solemn awe.

"An accomplished and amiable young woman, in the town of —, had been deeply affected by a sense of her spiritual danger. She was the only child of a fond and affectionate parent. The deep impressions which accompanied her discovery of guilt and depravity, awakened all the jealousies of the father. He dreaded the loss of that sprightliness and vivacity which constituted the life of his domestic circle. He was startled by the answers which his questions elicited; while he foresaw, or thought he foresaw, an encroachment on the hitherto unbroken tranquility of a deceived heart. Efforts were made to remove the cause of her disquietude; but they were such efforts as unsanctified wisdom directed. The Bible at last, oh how little may a parent knows the far reaching of the deed, when he snatches the word of life from the hand of a child! the Bible, and other books of true religion, were removed from her possession, and their place was supplied by works of fiction. An excursion of pleasure was proposed, and declined; an offer of gayer amusement shared the same fate; promises, remonstrances, and threatenings followed. But the father's infatuated perseverance at last brought compliance. Alas! how little may a parent be aware that he is adorning his offspring with the ornaments of eternal death, and leading them to the deadly sacrifice, like a follower of Moloch! The end was accomplished— all thoughts of piety, and all concern for the immortal future, vanished together. But oh, how in less than a year was the gaudy deception exploded! The fascinating and mirthful young girl was prostrated by a fever, that bade defiance to medical skill. The approach of death was unequivocal, and the countenance of every attendant fell, as if they had heard the flight of death's arrow. I see, even now, that look directed to the father, by the dying martyr of folly. The glazing eye was dim in hopelessness; and yet there seemed a something in its expiring rays that told reproof, and tenderness, and terror in the same glance. And that voice, its tone was decided, but sepulchral still, 'My father! Last year I would have sought the Redeemer. Father— your child is...' —Eternity heard the remainder of the sentence; for it was not uttered in time. In connection with this striking fact, read the following portions of Scripture. Matt. 5:10-12;

10:21-39; 1 Cor. 4:9-13; 2 Tim. 2:10-13; Heb. 10:23-39; 11; 1 Peter 1:6-9; 4:12-19; 2 Peter 2:20-22; Rev. 7:9-17.

4. *The discouragements of others lie nearer home still, they find them all in their own hearts.* The feeling with many is, that they make no progress; their views gain nothing in clearness, their convictions in depth, or their hearts in peace. They are neither more convinced, or more comforted; neither more spiritual, nor more decided than they were; and they are sometimes seized with fits of hopeless despondency, and are ready to give up the whole matter. Such a state of mind is very common, and a very perilous one, and affords ground for real alarm. Your duty and safety lie in considering that the fault is in yourself, and not in God. *You, you* are to blame. You are perhaps halting between two opinions. You are still probably endeavoring to compromise between religion and the world. You are not giving that fixed, devoted attention to the subject which it demands. You must, therefore, go afresh to the work. You must feel just like a man who has been swimming in a tide that is bearing him further from the shore, and who feels that it is necessary to make more vigorous efforts, or he is inevitably lost. *Give up!* No, anything but that. To perish now would be to perish terribly. While you are carrying on those heartless efforts, you may die—and in what a state!

But, perhaps, your complaints are the result of deep concern, which makes you *think there is no advance until you are really established in the full knowledge, faith, and hope of the gospel.* To this established state you ought to come, and to come without delay; and nothing hinders you from coming to it, but an evil heart of unbelief; and to this point I press you to come. But should your knowledge not grow as rapidly, nor your peace increase as solidly, as you expected or desired; should you feel yourself slow of growth in all that appertains to happy Christian experience; do not sink into a heartless and wretched frame, a kind of desponding pursuit of salvation, as of an object that you were never likely to obtain.

What you should do is immediately to repent, and believe the gospel; you cannot come to enlarged views and to settled peace without this. Going back, or giving up, is just the last thing you should think of. To turn back now, would be to turn back when near the cross! Look up, sinner! the stupendous object is before you; close by you; look up at the Crucified One! It is further back to your former state of indifference—than to the cross, the place of refuge. Just as you are, with no more knowledge, no more religious feeling, no more comfort—at once believe. Look up, I say, again, at the cross; it is distinctly visible to the eye of faith, from every point of the road along which you are journeying, and may be viewed any moment by him who will look that way. It is the sight of that dear object that will present every other in a right light, and invigorate every grace that belongs to true religion.

But may it not be, that your hindrances to a more rapid growth arise from some specific cause, some sin indulged, some corruption cherished? Is there not some sacrifice which you are unwilling to make, something which you are unwilling to surrender, although your judgment tells you the surrender ought to be made, and your conscience demands it? You *must* give up the forbidden thing, or your growth in grace is impossible. That one sin will, like a concealed worm at the root of a flower, eat out the very life of your piety, and cause it to droop, wither, and die!

Is it a companion, from whom you are unwilling to separate, but whose friendship is hindering your progress? And will you sacrifice your soul's salvation, heaven, and eternal glory, all that is dear to you as an immortal creature, and deliberately choose everlasting perdition—for that sin, or that friend? Take your choice between heaven and sacrifice, hell and present gratification. Immortal man! Pause and ponder—Can you hesitate? There is both awful guilt and imminent peril in every moment's delay. What if God should, as he justly may, send forth the command, "He is joined to idols; let him alone." Decide, then; decide at once! The moment in which you read this page may decide it—for if you are unwilling to give up your sinful practice or sinful companion, God may, from this moment, give you up to your idols!

But, perhaps, the slowness of your growth in knowledge and in grace may arise from another cause, I mean *your neglect of the promised influence and help of the Holy Spirit.* You have been too self-confident, and are now feeling the consequence of it. At one time, perhaps, your impressions were deep, your convictions strong, your frame of mind lively, and your feelings much excited; but you have allowed yourself to be seduced by Satan, who took advantage of those things, into a spirit of self-confidence and self-dependence. You have forgotten that in you there is no good thing; and have forsaken the fountain of living waters. You have never doubted the necessity of the Spirit's influence, but you have *neglected* it. You have grieved the Holy Spirit, and he has suspended that gracious aid which you so little valued. You have striven, but it has been in your own strength—and now you find that strength to be weakness itself. Now, then, profit by your error; and commit your soul, not only into the hands of Christ for pardon—but into the hands of the Spirit for sanctification. Now, lean upon that Divine power which works in us both to will and to do. Live in the Sirit; walk in the Spirit; pray in the Spirit; strive in the Spirit. Open your heart to his gracious influence; and let it be a *feeling*, as well as a conviction, that your spiritual life has no existence separate from his indwelling and inworking within you.

It may be, however, that this discouragement and complaint of a slow growth in religion are altogether unfounded, and are the result of disappointment, operating upon an humble or a morose mind. You may have expected at once to emerge from the thick darkness of an unconverted state, into the very noontide brightness of a full establishment in faith, hope, and love. You expected, probably, by one stride, or rather bound— to reach the position of experienced Christians. But, remember, that both in nature and in grace—the works of God come gradually to maturity. There is first the babe; then the young man; then the adult. What a feeble, glimmering spark of life is there sometimes in a new-born child; it is difficult to determine whether it is alive or dead; and even when unequivocal signs of life appear, what vigilant care is necessary to preserve the spark from being extinguished. Such has been the unpromising condition in which many a strong and long-lived man has commenced his existence. How analogous to this is the work of God in the soul.

So, again, with the growth of corn, there is first the blade; then the stalk; then the ear—and as it is in the field of nature, so is the growth of religion in the heart of man. We must not despise the "day of small things," either in ourselves or others, for God does not. It is said of our Divine Redeemer, "He will feed his flock like a shepherd." And in his flock there are lambs which can neither travel fast nor far. And what will he do with them? "He will gather the lambs in his arm, and carry them in his bosom." He will not carry them on his shoulder— the emblem of strength; but in his bosom—the image of tender love. "He will gently lead those who have their young." Those who are burdened with many fears and painful apprehensions.

How kindly did he forbear with the dullness, infirmities, and mistakes of his disciples; how gently did he correct the errors and sustain the minds of the two friends on their sad and gloomy walk to Emmaus, and keep alive the last glimmering spark of hope in their bosoms just when it was ready to expire. How graciously, in his addresses to the seven churches in Asia, did he mention all the good he could find among them, not overlooking even the "little strength" that was left in that of Philadelphia. Think of this, disheartened inquirer. Your dawn of knowledge shall shine brighter and brighter unto the perfect day; your infantile strength will grow to manly power; your tender blade of piety shall become the full ear of corn. You are looking to a Savior who "will not break the bruised reed, nor quench the smoking flax."

Weak grace is real grace, and is in connection with an infinite source in His fullness, who is the God of all grace, and who gives more grace. It is well to be humble, and to think lowly of your attainments; but remember, trees are not dead because they are not at once laden with fruit. I say not these things to paralyze your exertions after greater attainments, for he who is satisfied with the grace he has, has in reality none; but to check despondency, and prevent that disheartening sense of deficiency, which benumbs every exertion by extinguishing hope.

5. *Great discouragement has been experienced by others, on account of relapses and backslidings into actual sins.* It is, I admit, a grievous aggravation of sin, to fall into it after men have been awakened and convinced—and as there is much danger of this, the word of God contains many solemn warnings against it, which have been already referred to. We ought, therefore, to use the greatest watchfulness, and to present the most fervent prayers to be kept from these sins; and our vigilance should be doubled, in regard to those temptations to which we are most exposed from the peculiarity of our constitution, situation, or other circumstances. Yet sometimes even those who have sincerely and earnestly engaged in the pursuit of salvation have been, through a lack of watchfulness, betrayed again into sins from which they had been delivered. In such cases, the backslider, under the united influence of remorse and despondency, is apt to give up all for lost, and, un-

der the idea that he shall never obtain salvation, renounce the further pursuit of it.

Now I would say to such, that while you cannot be too deeply humbled for such relapses, you ought not to think that your case is desperate. If such sins could not be pardoned, and such sinners could not be restored, who then could be saved? But it is not so much a doubt of pardon for the past, you say, that discourages you, as a fear of preservation for the future. You find your heart so treacherous, your purposes so frail, your corruptions so strong, and your temptations so great; you have been so often victorious, and afterwards have been so often conquered, that you despair of success. What mean those desponding expressions? They seem to say, either that there is no help for you but in yourselves, or that God is not able to deliver you. Both are false. There *is* no help at all *in yourself*—but there is all-sufficient help *in God*. Take courage, sinner, take courage; God is almighty. Humble yourself under his mighty *hand* for the past, and then rise up and lean upon his mighty *arm* for the future. The blood of Christ can cleanse the conscience from the guilt of past sin, and the grace of the Holy Spirit can preserve you from the commission of *future sin* the backsliding can be forgiven, and the backslider himself restored, strengthened, confirmed, and made more than conqueror, as thousands have already been.

CHAPTER NINE

Cautions

1. *DO not seek to relieve your solicitude, or settle your religious peace, by making a profession of religion, and receiving the sacrament.* This is done by many people, who, after having remained for a long time in unrelieved solicitude, and after having tried all methods of gaining peace but the right one, determine to enter into church fellowship, and to receive the Lord's supper, with the hope of obtaining that comfort which they have hitherto sought in vain. But does not this look like a self-righteous dependence upon duties? In what way can the sacrament give relief to a burdened conscience? Is there anything more meritorious in that ordinance than in any other? Perhaps you say, that the emblems of the body and blood of our Lord will more deeply and powerfully impress the mind through the medium of the senses. So they will; but then the mind must be in a state of knowledge and faith to receive the impression—and I am now supposing that you are not yet in that state; that you have never yet committed your soul into the hands of Christ for full and free salvation. And in such a state of mind, to go to the sacrament or the church for peace is to expect that *they* can do that for you, which the work of Christ cannot do. Is not the blood of Christ able to take away your sins? Is anything necessary for your justification to be added to the righteousness of the Savior? What can

the sacrament do for you, if that be insufficient to save you? The sinner who seeks to lose his burden of guilt anywhere, whether it be in the prayer-meeting, or at the sacramental table, except at the cross of Christ, is in delusion. It is possible, nay probable, that by going to the Lord's supper you may feel for the time an abatement of your solicitude; your imagination may be excited; your feelings moved; and, mistaking this for faith, you may have peace; but it will be a false or a transient one. Either you will fall asleep in self-deception, or your concern will soon return, increased by an apprehension that you have added sin to sin, by receiving the Lord's supper in an unprepared state of mind.

This institution is intended, not to give peace to unbelievers, but consolation and edification to believers; not to bring us into a state of faith, but to be received in faith; not to remove the burden of sin from the conscience, but to keep in remembrance that Great Sacrifice by which the burden is removed. True it is, that God may reveal himself to the sinner in the breaking of bread; but the question is not what he may do, but what he may be expected to do—and even in case he does, what is it that relieves the conscience of its burden, and gives peace to the mind? Surely not the sacrament itself, but the great truth of Christ's sacrifice for sin, as set forth by it. I do not intend by these remarks to insist on the necessity of a full assurance of hope, as a necessary qualification for a right reception of the Lord's supper; but certainly there ought to be *real*, even if it be but weak, faith; for how else can we discern the Lord's body? Nothing, no, nothing, can give the guilty conscience peace, or take away our sins, but the atoning blood of Christ. And to pass by the cross of the Redeemer, without peace of mind, in the hope of finding it in the sacrament, is unquestionably to depend for acceptance with God upon our own religious duties, instead of the work of the Savior. The frame of mind in which we should receive the memorials of redeeming love, is that of a humble, thankful, and peaceful reliance upon the mediation of our Divine Lord for pardon and eternal life.

2. It is of great consequence, that in the early stages of your religious experience, *you should abstain as much as possible from a spirit of controversy.*

Your great concern is to find out the path of eternal happiness, and enter upon it. Salvation is your great object, or rather the way of obtaining it. Your cry is, "Life, eternal life;" and your course should be directly to the cross of the Redeemer. Nothing but what relates immediately to your reconciliation with God should be allowed to engage your attention. Do not allow your mind, then, to be diverted from such subjects as the new birth, or the justification of your soul before God—to the thorny controversies about baptism, church government, or even the doctrines of theology. Take up nothing controversially. The subjects of disputation are strong meat for adults, which will choke and destroy the babe in Christ; and even the former cannot feed much upon it, without having their spiritual health impaired, and their souls filled with rank and unhealthy distempers. Or, to change the metaphor, the man locked up in the condemned cell, under sentence of death, but who has hope of pardon, and is taking steps to obtain it, does not allow his mind to be drawn aside from his condition, by the questions which may be very properly discussed by the citizen and the patriot. If anyone were to carry him a newspaper, and endeavor to engage him as a partisan in some political strife, he would reply, with a look of astonishment that such topics should be intruded on his notice, "What are these matters to a man condemned to die? Assist me in gaining a pardon, and you will do me some service—but do not engage for such matters a moment of that time, which should be devoted to save me from death. When I am restored to liberty, I can think of politics, but not now."

So let the inquirer act, and say, in reference to those proselyting but injudicious zealots, who by controversy would meet and turn away the solicitude which is seeking the way to salvation. You can study these topics hereafter, but at present, "Stand in the way, and see, and ask for the old paths, where is the good way, and walk therein; and you shall find rest for your souls." Read your Bible and plain practical books, rather than controversial ones; be much in prayer and silent meditation; preserve a tranquil and unruffled mind, for it is in the stillness of devotional feeling, and the peace of holy reconciliation, and the quiet of untroubled thoughts, that the true light shines into the soul, and the small still voice of the Spirit of peace is heard. Many, adopting a different course, have plunged into the depths of controversy as soon as they became concerned about religion, and have lost charity in their professed pursuit after truth; and instead of becoming humble, holy, peaceful Christians, have turned out conceited, stormy, and restless polemics. In an early stage of their career the penitent was lost in the zealot; in their subsequent progress they took up with a religion of opinions, instead of pious feelings; and finished their course, it may be feared, not amidst the light and love of heaven, but in the world of 'unsanctified knowledge', where the devils believe and tremble.

3. It is necessary to caution you against *a spirit of curiosity,* as well as controversy.

You ought to seek after knowledge, as I have already stated. The Scripture abounds in admonitions on this head, and in reproofs to those who repose in indolence upon the lap of ignorance. Diligence in endeavors to grow in knowledge has the promise of success. "Then shall we know, if we follow on to know the Lord." But this is altogether distinct from a spirit of unhallowed curiosity. The temper which I am concerned to guard you against shows itself in various ways; sometimes *in rambling about from place to place of public worship.* In some cases, this arises from that restlessness and uneasiness of mind, which is common to people in their first religious experience. Like Noah's dove, they wander about, seeking rest, but find none; or, rather like a person in a fever, forgetting that the cause of disquietude is in themselves, they continually change their place, in the vain hope of obtaining that rest which can never come until their condition is altered. Finding no comfort under one preacher, they impute the blame to his sermons, and ramble off to another, under whose ministry they gain a little ease for a while; but merely by having their attention drawn away for a season from its usual track of thought. The novelty soon ceases, and he is forsaken for another, until they have gone the whole round of places within their reach; and they leave the last as far from peace as they were when they left the first.

Guard against this error, and learn that it is in Christ, and Christ alone, and not in any particular place of worship, or under any particular ministry, that you can find rest and peace. It is the glorious doctrine of a free, full, and present salvation in Christ, that must be the pillow of your poor aching and restless head, and not any particular manner or method of representing that doctrine.

But this rambling spirit is sometimes merely the eagerness of curiosity. Some young converts are ever to be seen in any place where anything out of the ordinary course is going on; they are to be seen at all times, all places, and all occasions, when and where a popular preacher is to be heard, or any of the stimulating varieties which abound in the religious world are to be found. This habit, however, is not friendly to the growth of religious feeling, or the progress of a work of grace in the soul. Even the public meetings of our religious institutions are not altogether the best atmosphere for infant piety to breathe. There is a tenderness, a delicacy, and a pensiveness, in the feelings of a mind recently awakened to a state of religious concern, which finds little that is congenial in the comparatively secular aspect of those assemblies. Eloquence and anecdote, as they are usually employed on such occasions, have but little that is calculated to deepen conviction, or relieve anxiety, but often much to diminish the one, and divert the other. If, indeed, our anniversaries were or could be conducted with that solemnity and seriousness which their object seems to require, then might inquirers after salvation attend them as one of the means of grace; but perhaps this can hardly be looked for, and therefore do I deliberately say to them, Do not at present attend such meetings too frequently; you ought rather to court retirement, to nurse reflection, to seek to grow in deeper seriousness, and to surrender yourselves to the dominion of conscience, and the teaching of God the Holy Spirit. Your present business is your own salvation; and when you have found that, and as one of the evidences of having found it, you must feel concerned for the salvation of others, and unite with your fellow-Christians in the various schemes of benevolent enterprise.

But curiosity may be indulged in another way, I mean a disposition to pry into the deep mysteries, the hidden things, the unrevealed secrets of God. Even the most established Christians, yes, the profoundest and most philosophic divines, may and do sometimes push their inquiries too far, and presumptuously put forth their hand to draw aside the veil of the holy of holies. But you especially should abstain from this; such questions as the origin of moral evil; the reconcileableness of God's foreknowledge with the freedom of man; the Divine decrees; the symbolical and unfulfilled prophecies, with other subjects of equal difficulty, are most unsuitable for you in your present state of mind. What you have to do with is, the simplest and plainest truths of the gospel. Your concern is, to obtain pardon, peace, and hope; and to do this you must not raise philosophic mists and clouds around the cross, but look at it as it is presented in the word of God; and as it there appears, clearly, simply, and alone. It has been said, that "in the Scripture there are depths in which an elephant may swim, and shallows which a lamb may ford." Your business is at present with the 'shallows', and to venture into the 'depths' is a perilous attempt, which I would not advise you to make.

4. *You should beware of setting up other standards of personal religion than the word of God, and making the religious*

experience of other Christians a test of the truth and reality of your own.

The Bible, and the Bible alone, is the true standard of godliness; and provided your views, feelings, and conduct are conformed to this, it is of no consequence that they do not harmonize exactly with what others experience. Not that there is any radical disagreement in the real piety of genuine Christians; but, with substantial agreement, there may be circumstantial differences; there may be unity of genus, yet variety of species. All true Christians love God, hate sin, feel Christ precious, give themselves to prayer, live holily; but they may not have been brought to this state by the same methods, or carry it forward to the same degree of perfection. In reading religious biography you will see great dissimilarity in the experience of God's people, and will be sometimes in danger of sinking into great distress, because you do not feel in all points as the saints did whose lives are before you. When you meet with instances of more than usual elevation of personal piety, of nearer approaches than common to perfection, do not conclude that you have no piety because you do not equal them, but rather see what you may become; be humbled that you are no more like them, and let their examples stimulate your energies, but not extinguish your hopes, or paralyze your efforts.

5. I caution you not to allow your convictions to be shaken, nor your mind to be staggered, by those instances of backsliding or apostasy which sometimes occur among professors of religion, and even such as were once accounted eminent professors.

It does, indeed, often give an solemn shock to the feelings and the steadfastness of inquirers, to witness the fall of those who once stood high in the estimation of believers, and the esteem of the world. Not a few, it is to be feared, have from that time gone back, and walked the ways of God no more. But how irrational, how guilty is such conduct! Did not Christ forewarn us to expect such instances, when he said, "Woe to the world because of offences, for it must needs be that offences come; but woe to that man by whom the offence comes" (Matt. 18:7). Such cases, therefore, are but the accomplishment of a prophecy, and prove, like other fulfilled predictions, the inspiration of Him by whom they were delivered. And they prove, in another way also, the Divine origin of the Christian religion; for if it had not been of God, it must have been destroyed long since by the misconduct of its professed friends, from which it has stood in far greater danger than from the enmity of its avowed foes. Counterfeits are a presumptive proof of the excellence of that which they profess to imitate, for who is at the trouble of imitating what is worthless? Do not, then, permit your mind to be affected by the conduct of false professors; at least, in any other way than that of deep grief that such things should occur to them; and of concerned, prayerful care, that they may never be repeated in you. Be this your supplication—

"Lord, let not all my hopes be vain,
Create my heart entirely new,
Which hypocrites could never attain,
Which false apostates never knew."

CHAPTER TEN

Encouragements to Inquirers

AMONG all the objects of human desire and pursuit, there is not one which we have so much encouragement to seek, or to hope for; there is not one, in reference to which despondency is so much out of place; there is not one, to which indubitable certainty so surely belongs, as the salvation of the soul, if it be sincerely desired, and scripturally sought for. The whole Bible is one vast encouragement to seek for eternal life; the death of Christ is another; and the existence and history of the church of God upon earth is a third. Men may despond of gaining wealth, or fame, or rank, or health; but no man out of hell need despond of gaining salvation. It is nearer to us, and more within our reach, than any other blessing we can name or think of. Our feelings in regard to earthly possessions can never rise higher than hope; but, in regard to salvation, they may take the character of certainty, provided we use the proper means.

1. It is one great source of encouragement, *that whatever difficulties lie in our way—all center in ourselves.*

God *will* not, and Satan and the world *cannot*, hinder our salvation. There is no obstacle which is in itself insurmountable; no enemy invincible; no objection unanswerable. If a

man had any other object in view, for the attainment of which
there existed no difficulty outside of himself, he would feel
greatly encouraged, and be ready to congratulate himself as
tolerably certain of success. Reader, the only difficulty in the
way of your salvation is in yourself. True it is, there are many
and great ones *there*, the least of which your own strength is
too weak to surmount; but the Lord God Omnipotent has engaged to you *his* power, if you are willing to be helped; and
therefore, in this view of the case, even your own weakness is
no insurmountable obstacle. The only question is, "Are you
sincerely willing and concerned to be saved?" Once made truly
willing, what is to hinder your salvation? Dwell again and
again on this simple idea, for it is full of encouragement. "The
only difficulty in my way to heaven is that which exists in my
own heart, and God is willing to remove that."

2. It is a great encouragement, *that God's mind is so full of
goodwill towards us, and that his heart is so set upon our salvation.*

If we had reason to suppose that *He* was unfriendly towards us; that he was reluctant to save us; that *His* mind was
upon the balance between friendship and hostility; that it need-
ed much importunity to entreat him to be merciful, and that he
granted us salvation unwillingly and grudgingly; this would indeed be discouraging, and might induce a fear that we should
not succeed. But the contrary is the fact. "God is love." "He is
gracious, and full of compassion." "God is rich in mercy;" and
"plenteous in mercy." He even "*delights* in mercy." "He is not
willing that any should perish, but that all should come to repentance." "He delights not in the death of a sinner, but would
rather that he should turn from his wickedness and live." Yes,
he confirms it by an oath, "As I live, says the Lord God, I have
no pleasure in the death of the wicked" (Eze. 33:11). Yes, it is
said that the salvation of sinners is so much his delight, that he

has engaged it *shall* be carried on—"the pleasure of the Lord *shall* prosper in his hands."

Now "by the pleasure of the Lord" we are to understand the salvation of sinners. Nor is this all, for it is affirmed that "the Lord takes pleasure in those who hope in his mercy" (Psa. 147:11). We cannot please him better, than by asking him to save us, and by expecting salvation at his hands. Now, inquirer, take this delightful view of God's dispensation towards you; for this is the right one. He is love; he has an infinite delight in making his creatures happy. It is true his love is a holy love, and therefore the more to be depended upon. Having made provision, in the gift and mediation of Christ, for saving you in a way consistent with his truth, and holiness, and justice, and thus removed every obstacle out of the way of the flowing forth of his love towards you—he is infinitely intent on saving and blessing you. All your dark, desponding thoughts of him are unjust, and injurious to his mercy. To conceive of him as unwilling to save you, is a slander upon his love; a false and foul calumny upon his grace. If he were with difficulty persuaded to save you, why did he give his Son to die for you? The salvation of your soul, the salvation of millions of souls, the salvation of the whole world, is not so great an act of love as the gift of Jesus Christ. After this you need not wonder at anything, nor doubt anything. "He who spared not his own Son, but delivered him up for us all, how shall he not with him also freely give us all things?" (Rom 8:32). You have God's mind, and heart, and purpose, and attributes, all on the side of your salvation; and is not this encouragement enough?

3. Consider *the mind, character, and work of our Lord Jesus Christ.*

He came on purpose to save sinners; he has done everything necessary for their salvation; he is able to save *to the uttermost;* he has invited all to him for salvation; he has promised to save them—and do you think he will now fail? Think of the glory of his person, God manifest in the flesh; think of the design of his incarnation, sufferings, and death; think of the perfection of his work in satisfying Divine justice, magnifying the law, sustaining the moral government of God in all its purity, dignity, and effectiveness; think of the love of his heart, the power of his arm, and the connection between his mediatorial renown and the salvation of sinners; think of his universal dominion over angels, devils, men, nature, providence; think of his continued and prevailing intercession at the right hand of God; think of his universal invitations, and his absolute promises. What topics these, what sources of encouragement! How much is his heart fixed upon the salvation of sinners! This was the joy that was set before him, and for which he endured the cross, despising the shame; this is the travail of his soul, and by it its ineffable longings will be satisfied. Your salvation is his business, and the accomplishment of it will be his reward. If he could be conceived to be indifferent to your salvation, will he be indifferent to his own glory? Will he belie his own name, and destroy his own work, and falsify his promises, and throw away his own reward, and impair his own renown as a Savior, by refusing to save you? Is it probable? Is it possible?

4. *Dwell upon the infinite and all-sufficient resources of the Holy Spirit.*

This Divine Agent is as omnipotent to sanctify, as the power of God was in the beginning to create the heavens and the earth. If you were cast upon your own resources, you might well exclaim, "Who is sufficient for these things?" and abandon the hope of salvation for fixed and remediless despair. But the economy of redemption provides no less for the effectual *application* of its benefits by the work of the Holy Spirit, than it does for the *procurement* of them by the mediation of Christ; and the claims of the Godhead were not more completely foreseen and provided for by the latter, than all the weakness, poverty, and wickednesses of the human heart, were foreseen and provided for also by the former. There is a glorious completeness in the scheme of redemption; even the suspicious eye of unbelief, and the searching look of a troubled and anxious conscience, can find no defect in it. The blindness of your judgment; the hardness and deceitfulness of your heart; the perversity of your will; the deadness of your conscience; the wildness of your imagination; the disorder of your passions; your backwardness to good; your proneness to evil; your irresoluteness; your timidity; your fickleness; all, all have been foreseen and provided for, in the inexhaustible riches of grace in the blessed Spirit of God. On those riches you are encouraged to rely and to draw, without measure and without end. You are not required to act, to speak, to will, to feel, to think, except in dependence on that Divine Agent. You are commanded to look to him for every variety of operation, and for every degree of influence, and for every timely putting forth of his power and wisdom, that the exigency of your circumstances may require. Read especially the following passages of Scripture, and ask if there be not encouragement enough in them? Luke 11:9-13; Rom. 8:10-17; James 1:5, 6; Gal. 5:22, 23; John 16:7-11; 2 Cor. 12:9, 10.

5. *Dwell upon the general complexion of the word of God*, as so largely made up of commands to seek salvation; invitations to accept of it; promises to insure it; and descriptions, setting forth its blessings in their vastness, variety, suitableness, and certainty.

If the whole Bible were to be summed up in one short comprehensive sentence, it would be this—*"This is a faithful saying, and worthy of all acceptance, that Christ Jesus came into the world to save sinners, of whom I am chief."* Or, reducing it still more, it would all be contained in that one word, of immense, infinite, and eternal import, *Salvation*. Everything in the Bible tends to this as its center—here all the lines of history and prophecy, of the Old Testament and the New, of the law and the gospel meet. Salvation glimmers amidst the clouds and shadows of the Levitical economy, and shines forth in all its glory from the facts of the Christian dispensation. It was the subject that dropped in sweet but mystic accents from the lips of Mercy on the despairing minds of our first parents; it was the subject which was hinted in the softer tones of the ceremonial law, when the thunders of the decalogue had ceased to terrify the affrighted Israelites at Sinai; it was the subject to which the prophet struck his harp, it was fore shadowed in the Psalms of David, and the enraptured ecstasies of Isaiah; it was the subject which angels sang on the night of Christ's nativity; it was the subject which evangelists recorded in their histories, and apostles described in their epistles; and which even the solemn visions of the Apocalypse seem designed to magnify and illustrate, by representing it as the point of harmony between heaven and earth, and the link that connects the events of time with the glories of eternity. The Bible, then, inquirer, presents salvation to your attention, and employs all its fullness to attract, all its authority to command, and all its graciousness to invite you, to its pursuit; and even uses its threatenings and its thunders for the merciful purpose of driving you for refuge to the hope set before you in the gospel. Is not this encouragement?

6. *The unchangeableness of God's nature and covenant,* is a source of boundless hope.

He has invited, he has commanded, he has promised; and he is not a man that he should lie, nor the son of man that he should repent; but he is the Father of lights, with whom there is no variableness, nor shadow of a change. Immutable in his nature, he is equally so in his purpose and in his promise. Whom he loves, he loves to the end. Could you examine the secret lists of his friends, you would find neither blots nor erasures there.

"We know that all things work together for good for those who love God, to those who are called according to his purpose. For whom he foreknew, he also predestined to be conformed to the image of his Son, that he might be the firstborn among many brothers. Whom he predestined, those he also called. Whom he called, those he also justified. Whom he justified, those he also glorified. What then shall we say about these things? If God is for us, who can be against us? He who didn't spare his own Son, but delivered him up for us all, how would he not also with him freely give us all things? Who could bring a charge against God's chosen ones? It is God who justifies. Who is he who condemns? It is Christ who died, yes rather, who was raised from the dead, who is at the right hand of God, who also makes intercession for us. Who shall separate us from the love of Christ? Could oppression, or anguish, or persecution, or famine, or nakedness, or peril, or sword? Even as it is written, "For your sake we are killed all day long. We were accounted as sheep for the slaughter." No, in all these things, we are more than conquerors through him who loved us. For I am persuaded, that neither death, nor life, nor angels, nor principalities, nor things present, nor things to come, nor powers, nor height, nor depth, nor any other created thing, will be able to separate us from the love of God, which is in Christ Jesus our Lord" (Romans 8:28-39).

Sublime language! Triumphant boast! Inspired and inspiring exultation! Heaven heard it, and approved; hell heard it, and trembled; and let saints on earth hear it, and rejoice. Inquirer, be comforted; where a good work is begun in the heart, it shall be carried on until the day of Jesus Christ (Phil. 1:6). The Spirit, who builds for himself a temple in the soul of man, will not leave it unfinished, nor allow it to sink to ruins after he has finished it. Though enemies without may oppose and ridicule, and though enemies within may stir up occasional insurrection and interruption, the work *shall* go on, until the topstone shall be brought forth amidst the shouts of "Grace, grace!" The purpose of God must stand, in spite of all the force or fraud, the power and malice of earth and hell combined. Is not this encouragement?

7. *Consider the sympathies and prayers of fellow Christians.*

Discouraged as you may have been by the indifference and lukewarmness of *some*, let it comfort you to know that all are not thus. There are myriads of holy ministers of Christ, and millions of pious men and women from age to age, pouring out their fervent supplications to God, for those who are inquiring the way to Zion with their faces pointed there. Have you not heard your case borne with tenderness, and minuteness, and earnestness, upon the hearts of your friends and by your ministers? Have you not thus found the feelings of the assembly poured in a full tide of sympathy into your heart? Yes, and not only do the "Spirit and the bride say, Come," in this *public* manner—not only does the voice of *united* prayer commend you to God; but, in thousands of closets of praying men, you are commended to God, and Divine grace is implored on your souls. In those sad and solemn moments, when you are disheartened and ready to faint, when, instead of prayer, you can send forth nothing but groanings which cannot be uttered, then think, with pleasure and with hope, upon the many intercessors who are praying for you, and "thank God, and take courage."

8. Take encouragement from the consideration of *the ministry of angels;* for "are they not all ministering spirits, sent forth to minister to those who shall be heirs of salvation?" What offices they perform we know not, perhaps because it is not safe for us to know; why they are employed we know not; or what is the extent of our obligation we know not—but the bare fact that such instruments *are* employed about you, such attendants are engaged upon your interests, such spectators are

witnessing you, such friends are sympathizing with you, is a sweetly pleasing and encouraging idea. They have already rejoiced over your conversion, if indeed you *are* converted; and have had you consigned to their care, to minister to your welfare. You may be despised by men, but you are regarded by angels; you may be neglected by men, but you are attended by angels; you may be dismissed by men, but you are associated with angels; you may be opposed and persecuted by men, but angels are ministering spirits, sent forth to minister unto your salvation. Is not this encouragement?

9. Consider how many who were once tried, disheartened, weak, as you are now, have been carried in safety through all their difficulties, and are now before the throne of God in glory everlasting.

The apostle John seems to have set open the doors of the heavenly temple, that the sights within might beam upon our eyes, and the sounds resound on our ears. "After these things I looked, and behold, a great multitude, which no man could number, out of every nation and of all tribes, peoples, and languages, standing before the throne and before the Lamb, dressed in white robes, with palm branches in their hands. They cried with a loud voice, saying, 'Salvation be to our God, who sits on the throne, and to the Lamb!'"(Rev. 7:9,10). And who are they that send forth such strains? Who are they, and from where did they come? "These are those who came out of the great tribulation. They washed their robes, and made them white in the Lamb's blood. Therefore they are before the throne of God, they serve him day and night in his temple. He who sits on the throne will shelter them with his presence. They will never be hungry, neither thirsty any more; neither will the sun beat on them, nor any heat; for the Lamb who is in the midst of the throne shepherds them, and leads them to springs of waters of life. And God will wipe away every tear from their eyes." *They* were once upon earth; once men of like passions with yourself; once beginning their religious course as you now are;

> "Once they were mourning here below,
> And wet their couch with tears—
> They wrestled hard, as we do now,
> With sins, and doubts, and fears."

There is not a burden that oppresses *your* heart, but oppressed theirs; there is not a fear that agitates your mind, but agitated theirs; there is not a temptation that assails you, but assailed them; there is not an obstacle that terrifies you, but terrified them; they were once as ignorant, as weak, as sinful, as timid, as discouraged, as you are now; there is not a sorrow, a perplexity, or a danger with which you are painfully familiar, but they passed through before you. But there they are in heaven, more than conquerors over all these things, through him who loved them. He who saved them has engaged to save *you*; nor is his ear heavy, nor his arm shortened. "Therefore, since we are surrounded by so great a cloud of witnesses, let us also lay aside every weight, and sin which clings so closely, and let us run with endurance the race that is set before us, looking to Jesus, the founder and perfecter of our faith, who for the joy that was set before him endured the cross, despising the shame, and is seated at the right hand of the throne of God" (Heb. 12:1,2).

10. *Let the magnitude of the blessing you are seeking, and the prospect of its consummation in eternal glory, encourage you.*

You are seeking *salvation*, a word which none but the mind of God can comprehend, for it includes, as I have already said, what is infinite and eternal. It will bless you for both worlds, this and the next. In the present life, it will bestow upon you the pardon of all your sins; the justification of your person; the renewal and sanctification of your nature; adoption into the family of God; the Spirit of adoption. It will be the guardian of your reputation; the protector of your property; an auxiliary to your health; a spring of comfort in the dreariest situation; a light in the darkest scene of distress; a companion in the deepest solitude; a counselor in every perplexity; a help in weakness; a check in temptation; it will associate you with the redeemed and holy people of God; conduct you in honor through the changing scenes of life; attend you to the verge of eternity; soften your dying pillow; assuage the agony of separation; and cheer you amidst the agonies of death, with the hopes of immortality.

And all this is but the prelude, the pledge, and the foretaste of what awaits you beyond the grave! What *that* is, should be told only in the words of the Spirit of God; for "Eye has not seen, nor ear heard, neither has entered into the heart of man—the things which God has prepared for those who love him." "Father," said our Lord, "I will that they also, whom you have given me, be with me where I am, that they may behold my glory." "So shall we ever be with the Lord." "He who believes on the Son has everlasting life." "To them who, by patient continuance in well-doing, seek for glory and honor and immortality, eternal life." "Our light affliction, which is but for a moment, works for us a far more exceeding and eternal weight of glory; for the things which are not seen are eternal." "Who has begotten us to an inheritance incorruptible, and undefiled, and that fades not away, reserved in heaven for you, who are kept by the power of God through faith unto salvation, ready to be revealed in the last time." "It does not yet appear what we shall be; but we know that when He shall appear, we shall be like him, for we shall see him as he is."

"After these things I looked, and behold, a great multitude, which no man could number, out of every nation and of all tribes, peoples, and languages, standing before the throne and before the Lamb, dressed in white robes, with palm branches in their hands. They cried with a loud voice, saying, "Salvation be to our God, who sits on the throne, and to the Lamb!" All the angels were standing around the throne, the elders, and the four living creatures; and they fell on their faces before his throne, and worshiped God, saying, "Amen! Blessing, glory, wisdom, thanksgiving, honor, power, and might, be to our God forever and ever! Amen." One of the elders answered, saying to me, "These who are arrayed in white robes, who are they, and from where did they come?" I told him, "My lord, you know." He said to me, "These are those who came out of the great tribulation. They washed their robes, and made them white in the Lamb's blood. Therefore they are before the throne of God, they serve him day and night in his temple. He who sits on the throne will shelter them with His presence. They will never be hungry, neither thirsty any more; neither will the sun beat on them, nor any heat; for the Lamb who is in the midst of the throne shepherds them, and leads them to springs of waters of life. And God will wipe away every tear from their eyes." (Revelation 7:9-17)

Anxious inquirer after salvation, take courage, look upward to heaven, and onward to eternal glory, and see what you are seeking, and what you are encouraged to expect!

MORE FROM
C.C.R. Publishing

That Christ May Have Preeminence
Various Authors:
*Isaac Ambrose, Samuel Davies, Thomas Watson, Octavius
Winslow, Jonathan Edwards, Richard Sibbes, John Flavel and
Thomas Chalmers*
242 pages | ISBN: 978-1484998465

The School of Calvary & The Passion For Souls
Author: John Henry Jowett
142 pages | ISBN: 978-1494878931

Printed in Great Britain
by Amazon